MEET

MW01199990

Normal Sex & Home in three days. Don't wash.

Samuel Ace
Linda Smukler

Belladonna*
Germinal Texts 3

Introduction

Dear Linda:

The time is late. It's almost 10:00 pm. You are with me today in a classroom at the women's college where I teach. My friend, Zoë Tuck, and I are presenting our work to a colleague's Queer & Trans writing workshop. That this class exists at all is in itself a miracle. Historically, women's colleges have been a relatively safe place for those who were gender non-conforming, although those individuals were often un-named and unrecognized. Today, in this classroom, I am surrounded by young students who proudly name themselves as trans, queer, non-binary, gender non-conforming, and by other terms to describe their gender identities.

It's been over five years since the publication of *Troubling the Line: Trans and Genderqueer Poetry and Poetics*.[1] Classes like this one are more and more common on campuses around the country. Trans- and gender non-conforming-identified writers are ever more visible and publishing. Although that visibility is still marginalized, every time I encounter a younger writer who writes openly about the complexity of gender, I am utterly grateful.

I have projected your picture on a screen. I have talked about our books, yours and mine. I have spoken about your childhood, your schooling, your young adulthood in New York. I have described how your sister could sing the C major scale correctly, in contrast to the way your notes came out of your throat quietly and out of tune, heading down the scale instead of up. I've shared that you were nearly blind in one eye and wore thick glasses with prisms. That your mother tied your hair into a ponytail. That you wore black and white saddle shoes that were always scuffed and dirty. I recounted how you hated dresses and the concert gowns you had to wear when you played the piano in recitals, and how embarrassed those dresses made you feel. As I spoke, I switched easily between the first person, calling you *I* and *me*, and the third, using your name and the pronouns *she* and *her*.

I know I have created a kind of binary here. It is simply a contrivance, a schema, that allows me to address you. I've decided to keep the armature for now, imperfect as it is.

Dear friend who is me and no longer me, dear love who I have never left behind, dear gorgeous *Linda*, in all that your name implies, let me say again that I love you.

5

Dear Sam:

When I close my eyes and think about you and me, it is you I see, and who I always see when I look in the mirror. No need for apologies. In my mid-twenties, my head nearly shaved, I often wore a long-sleeved white button-down shirt with baggy men's wool pants held up by suspenders. By the late '70s, early '80s, my wardrobe, purchased at thrift stores near my apartment in Manhattan's East Village, included a Sam Spade-like fedora that was the origin of your name, which was then only a nickname. A few years later, when I started to read poetry in public, I performed in suits bought at a close-out sale on 1st Avenue—boys' suits from the '60s, with tight pant legs, flat fronts, and jackets with narrow lapels. I bought more than one. They fit my small frame and seemed to perfectly repre-sent the gender presentation I desired—boyish and somewhat nymph-like. Underneath, I wore a black t-shirt or button-down shirt, over another t-shirt, usually white.

I was born nearly blind in one eye, so near-sighted that I was unable to see further than the hands in front of my face. At age three, I wore an eye-patch and glasses. When and where did I first see a boy? I understood that my sister was a girl, but how did I understand what a boy was enough to want to be one? Was my desire innate? Was it shaped by the first picture books my parents read to me as a toddler? The tv had a special screen that was designed to force me, without the patch, to use both of my eyes together. But the images would rarely fuse. I would squint my right eye, only to see Lassie on the left side of the screen, staring right, seeming to communi-cate with someone behind a grey wall. If I squinted my left eye, Lassie would disappear, but there was Timmy talking to his mother. Timmy was a pale white boy with blonde hair who lived on a farm. I was a pale white girl with brown hair and a ponytail who lived in a little house in a white suburb on the east side of Cleveland. Timmy did not seem to have any friends except his dog, and both of them could go out of the house and into the forest or across the fields any time they wanted. I did not have any friends, but I had a dog. I knew only a little about fields or forests. I wanted to be Timmy. I secretly called myself Timmy. I imagined I had short hair like his, that I wore his jeans. I thought up many adventures. Already I had a different idea of myself than my mother had of me. As I watched Timmy's mother comfort him when he came home from being lost, I wanted her to be my mother. This was my dream. It looked different from what was happening in my house, even as only half a picture.

It made my mother so happy when I performed you, Linda, with long hair, sitting down at the piano in a velvet dress, playing Debussy and Beethoven. Perhaps she saw a version of herself in me and my sisters. She wanted us to succeed, to be excellent in all ways: at music, at family, at beauty, at intellect, at marriage. Her aspirations for us were persistent, fierce, and brutal. But in my earliest memories, I yearned, mostly in secret, for you, Sam. With a sharp pencil, I carved you into the baseboard of the living room piano where I had to practice. I lied about the vandalism and was punished severely for both the lie and the destruction, but I continued to carve my totems. I went to sleep dreaming of you. I tried out many names for you. I hope you remember that I was called Sam long before you legally changed our name.

Dear Linda,

It's been more difficult than I expected to write this essay. How does a writer look back? What, or better *who*, will they find there? Who was it who wrote the words on the page? Reading through *Normal Sex* and *Home in three days. Don't wash.*, I am faced with a person I no longer fully recognize. I am a different creature, not only in name and appearance, but as a human being and a writer. Linda, I see your courage and your anger. I see you writing about childhood, alcohol, obsession, and rigid familial relationships warped by the reach of generational traumas. The act of writing these stories fixes them in time. Unlike actual people and relationships, these portraits do not evolve.

Today, I see my family and myself with more compassion than you possibly could have felt thirty-something years ago. I see a mother terrified of slipping back into where she came from, her abuse and the conservative dreams of her parents. Maybe you had similar fears, a need to break away, to clarify, to channel your past and your loves into your poems.

I wish I could find your old suits in my closet. I don't think they would fit, but I dress not so differently than you did then. My shoulders are slightly wider, and although my feet have grown a bit, my small shoe size is still somewhat difficult to find.

I look at myself in the mirror and see a face not unlike my father's. He never grew a beard, but like him, and many of my male relatives, I am going bald. I am no longer mistaken for a boy, or even a young man. On the street, I am often seen as an older white man, though every once in a while, my beard hidden inside a thick winter scarf and coat, along with my short stature and small frame, I am taken for a woman.

I started gender-related therapy when I moved to Tucson in 1997. I fought the idea of physical transition for years, struggling to reach some internal peace and acceptance of the gender I was assigned at birth. But the question that began in my childhood continued to haunt me. I simply could not find resolution. In 2000, I finally began a medical transition. Once I made that decision and took steps to manifest it in my life, it was as if the question of my gender lifted off my shoulders and disappeared. The constant back and forth, the projections, the fears, the endless pro and con lists, the theoretical what ifs, simply stopped. The issues I spent a lifetime trying to analyze and solve suddenly dematerialized. My interest in the *idea* of gender did not go away, but it was as if an enormous space opened up around my entire being when I finally stopped trying to figure out what to do and instead put my feet on the ground and started to walk.

I continued to write but published rarely in the aughts. Looking back, I wonder how much this had to do with the relationship of my body to the writing, always so intimately tied to the physical, to placing my hands on a typewriter or computer keyboard as I once put my fingers on the piano. In moving to the Southwest from the Northeast, I believe I needed to find home in my physical location, as well as in my transforming body. As one way of finding home, I spent much of my creative energy traveling and camping all over Arizona, Utah, and New Mexico in an old Toyota Previa, taking slow photographs of the unfamiliar landscape with an antiquated large-format camera I bought off of eBay. Through my physical transition, I was becoming concrete, not just a story I told myself. The writing came more easily as I settled into the desert and became somatically more solid in myself.

8

Dear Sam:

My hands were shaking with excitement and gratitude when I took out that first slim blue copy of *Normal Sex* from the cardboard box sent to me by Nancy Bereano at Firebrand Books. It was the spring of 1994 and I was living and teaching on the border of the Taconics and the Berkshires, in Columbia County, NY, near Edna St. Vincent Millay's home and the Millay Colony, where I had enjoyed a couple of writing residencies. The book contained the collected "Tales of a Lost Boyhood," first begun in a workshop led by Gloria Anzaldúa in her apartment in Sunset Park, Brooklyn. I was there with Nina and Roz, and others whose names I no longer recall. But I remember their presence and Gloria's, the warmth with which they all held me, and held each other, in those early stages of our writing lives.

My family had known for some time that a book was in the works, but had never asked to read it. When they did finally ask, a month before publication, my wishful thinking imagined a scene not unlike those experienced by certain writer friends, whose families, proud of accomplishment, would display their offspring's book on a coffee table without much worry about content. Despite my fantasy, I hesitated to give my family the book. In the end, I decided to go ahead, knowing they would see it sooner or later.

I was visiting New York in early March when my mother called to ask if I would join her and my father for breakfast at their apartment. When I arrived, pastries in hand, I found a darkened room, the shades drawn against the sunny morning. I was met not only by my parents, but by my two sisters, one of whom greeted me with an accusatory *How could you?*

I froze. This was to be no casual breakfast. I sat down, already numb. Apparently, they had all read the book. My sisters and mother did most of the talking, while my father stayed mostly silent. They told me that unless I stopped the publication, I would never be welcome in the family again. I felt I had to argue, to speak about the difference between fiction and non-fiction, to somehow let them know I meant no harm. One of my sisters said: *You write so well, why do you have to write about such ugliness? Why can't you write about nature and beauty?* In defense, I replied: *I do write about nature and beauty.* My words only sounded like sarcasm. I *did* write about beauty. And love, and abjection, abuse and apple trees and fields, bodies and sex and mud, the birds that sing on New York City mornings. My words had no effect. My family was beyond hearing.

I should have known what would happen. The publication of the book wasn't the first time they had stopped speaking to me: they had done so for a few years when I first came out to them as lesbian; then again when they read my earlier writing, some of which was published in *Normal Sex*. The stories in the poems were fictionalized, some inspired by real events, some invented. I not only wrote about a gender non-conforming child, lesbian desire, and incest, but also about individuals in a family that held deep secrets. In the face of my mother's own family history, this was not the representation of a family she had worked so hard to construct in order to hold herself and those closest to her together.

Some minor, but profoundly consequential errors arose in the course of the publication. First, the publisher left out my dedication to Gloria. Second, I had included a standard disclaimer in the book: *The poems, stories, all names, characters, and incidents portrayed in this book are fictitious. No identification with actual persons (living or deceased), places, buildings, and products is intended or should be inferred.* The publisher also neglected to include the disclaimer. But I wonder if those mere words, had they appeared, would have made any difference to my parents or my siblings.

Dear Linda:

Even though I'm currently enjoying the back and forth of these letters, I want to locate myself with you, integrated and whole. A few years ago, I wrote a series of epistolary poems that began with the salutations *Dear L* and *Dear S*. Some were actually published in that form. But the more I worked on the poems, the difference between our voices became less discernable and more of an internal conversation. I eventually decided to remove the salutations, uncomfortable with a split between a *you* and a *me*. Unlike what was happening in those poems, I'm listening more carefully to you today, wanting your voice to be more fully present in the world.

Today I am back in the Northeast, sitting in a green chair I bought for my partner, looking out of the window at an old mill building on the banks of a river in a New England town. My partner sits on the couch across from me. He goes by the pronoun *he*, as do I. In so many ways, he brought me to this place, this moment, this cold March morning, gazing out through the sunlight and the nascent spring, to the windows across the street. Half building, half sky.

My family's shunning wasn't permanent. One day in 2001, seven years after *Normal Sex* was published, and a year after I had started my physical transition in Tucson, I received a card from my mother saying that she and my father wanted to visit. Surprised, but ever optimistic, I invited them to stay with me and my former partner at our house. They declined, stating they were only visiting for a day, and would instead get a room in a hotel.

They arrived late in the evening, and my partner and I met them at their hotel. My father gave me a warm hug, and I hugged him back, feeling close to tears at the loss of so many years. When I went to hug my mother, she turned away and said: *I'm not ready for that yet*, her hands shaking and her face rigid. She did however manage to comment on my sparse moustache, pointing to my face and saying: *Ewwww. What's that?* I immediately stepped back, feeling an old coldness inside my chest. Although I had written to let them know about my transition, I knew it was a shock for my mother, after so many years, to see hair on my face. We quickly left to find a restaurant and, once seated, I watched my mother's hands stop shaking the moment she held a deep glass of scotch to her lips.

Over the next many years, my parents quietly let me back into their lives, my father more than my mother. He began to call me every couple of weeks, and when he didn't, I would call him. He wanted to talk about our work, politics, books, and even writing. One of the last times I saw him, he invited me to his office, where he introduced me to his colleagues as his son.

Later I found out that my parents told almost no one that we had a relationship. They had kept our visits, our dinners, our phone calls, completely siloed off from the rest of their lives. This included any relationship with my sisters, who continued to shun me and keep me from any contact with my nieces and nephews. In a waiting room at the hospital where my father was dying, his brother told me he had been given the impression that I simply had moved away and refused to speak to the family, rather than the other way around. After my father's death, only his closest cousin told me he had expressed to her how important our relationship was to him and how happy he was that we were in close contact. She was the only extended family member who seemed to know this.

Dear Sam:

The seeds of "Tales of a Lost Boyhood" first appeared in Gloria's living room, where she spoke deeply to us about memory, transition, and transformation. Later, she wrote:

Each piece of writing I do creates or uncovers its own spirit, a spirit that manifests itself through words and images. Imagination takes fragments, slices of life and experiences that seem unrelated, then seeks their hidden connections and merges them into a whole. I have to trust this process. I have to serve the forces/spirits interacting through me that govern the work. I have to allow the spirits to surface. Nepantla, el lugar entremedios, is the space between body and psyche where image and story making takes place, where spirits surface. When I sit and images come to me, I am in my body but I'm also in another place, the space between worlds (nepantla). Images connect the various worlds I inhabit or that inhabit me.
    [...]
    *The path of the artist, the creative impulse, what I call the **Coyolxauhqui imperative** is basically an attempt to heal the wounds. It's a search for inner completeness. Suffering is one of the motivating forces of the creative impulse. Adversity calls forth your best energies and most creative solutions. Creativity sets off an alchemical process that transforms adversity and difficulties into works of art. All of life's adventures go into the cauldron, la oya, where all fragments, inconsistencies, contradictions are stirred and cooked to a new integration. They undergo transformation.*
    *For me esta oya is the **body**. I have to inhabit the body, discover its sensitivity and intelligence. When all your*

12

*antenna quiver and your body becomes a lightning rod, a
radio receiver, a seismograph detecting and recording ground
movement, when your body responds, every part of you moves
in synchronicity. All responses to the world take place within
our bodies. Our bodies are tuning forks receiving impressions,
which in turn activate other responses. An artist has to stay
focused on the point of intersection (nepantla) between inner
and outer worlds through her senses. Listening to an inner
order, the voice of real intuition, allows it to come through
the artist's body and into the body of the work. The work will
pass on this energy to the reader or viewer and feed her or his
soul. The artist transmits and transforms inner energies and
forces, energies and forces that may come from another realm,
another order of intelligence. These forces use la artista to
transmit their intelligence, transmit ideas, values that awaken
higher states of consciousness. Once conocimiento (aware-
ness) is reached, you have to act in the light of your knowl-
edge. I call this spiritual activism.*[2]

As I sat in the low warm light of Gloria's apartment, I began
to make a practice of letting the physicality of the body lead
and become the writing. I came to trust Gloria and the other
students in the class. I was getting to know Nina, who like me,
was softly masculine. Gloria taught us to simply write without a
script or judgment. She encouraged us to write from our bod-
ies, to journey across into the unknown. I no longer remember
what I wrote first, but with her prompting, I began to excavate
the sensory and emotional realities of my childhood, including
my imaginary boyhood.

After every workshop, several of us went to an Irish
bar down the street. There I drank to soothe the terror of what
I had allowed myself to unearth in that living room. Dollar for a
shot. Fifty cents for a chaser of beer. Afterwards, I took the train
back to my little apartment, where I drank more before bed.

My landlord refused to fix the boiler and I often had
no heat or hot water. The two white gay boys across the way,
one of whom was the building manager, regularly beat each
other. Upstairs, my white neighbor ritually beat up his white
girlfriend so badly that, one day, hearing screams, I called the
police. With deep scratches and blood on her face, the girl-
friend told the police that nothing had happened and that she

was fine. The next day she came to my door and screamed at me for interfering. To write something to take to Brooklyn the following week, I would sit at a small desk in my tiny 8' x 8' study, shelves of books to my back, close my eyes, and try to shut out what was happening in the rest of the building. I could write feverishly for 10 or 15 minutes, then would need to reward myself with a scotch and a cigarette. I would repeat that routine over and over again until eventually I passed out.

　　　　To support myself, I did layout at a typesetting shop at 5th Avenue and 14th Street. The job barely paid the rent, but in New York, lesbian and gay literature was becoming more visible. I first heard Gloria and so many other queer writers at Carl Morse's *Open Lines* reading series at the Judson Memorial Church. I eventually read there and at venues like the WOW Café where Peggy Shaw and Lois Weaver held court. The Lesbian Herstory Archives became my library. Small presses were publishing monographs by lesbian and gay poets whose work was previously self-published. In the states, the first gay and lesbian anthologies were emerging, including, among others, Joan Larkin and Elly Bulkin's *Lesbian Poetry: An Anthology* (1981),[3] Barbara Smith's *Home Girls: A Black Feminist Anthology* (1983),[4] and Gloria Anzaldúa and Cherríe Moraga's *This Bridge Called My Back: Writings of Radical Women of Color* (1983).[5] In 1986, Joseph Beam published *In the Life: A Black Gay Anthology*,[6] and Larkin and Morse published *Gay and Lesbian Poetry in Our Time* (1988)[7] at the exact time in New York when AIDS was in the midst of its ascendant and seemingly unstoppable trajectory.

Dear Linda:

Can we talk about those myths of masculinity that you wrote about? Your nostalgia for a boyhood? Those myths seem to form the subtext of the "Tales," at least as I understand them today, sitting in my partner's chair looking out at the sun. It's 9 a.m. on March 31st. Trans Day of Visibility. I am in my living room hearing cars pass by. Am I visible? Are you? Today my beard is turning white and I've been sober, as of two days ago, for 32 years, almost half my life. We were born squarely at the mid-point of the last century in Cleveland, Ohio. I am living what

14

seems to be a shorter and shorter life. We were descendants of Jewish survivors from Europe, where many of our ancestors were killed nearly a decade before we appeared. Great-grandparents, cousins, uncles, aunts, all murdered. People we would never know, from villages and cities we would never know. Today we still live in a country and world plagued by despots and autocrats, wracked by racism, torn apart by rapacious capitalism. When I walk down the street, I often pass as a white cis-male, far more protected from violence than those in my community who are black, brown, gender non-conforming and, most vulnerable, trans women of color.

Does it make sense to you that today I am grateful I did not have a boyhood? Some of my cis-male friends have shared with me harsh depictions of their childhoods. Some were beaten, hazed, and humiliated. Some competed viciously with each other. Some bonded over cruelty. Some valorized strength and daring and could not tolerate vulnerability. Their boyhoods were not like Timmy's. They did not have a dog who solved their problems. I believe that you, as a child, had little understanding of any of this.

It's clear to me how deeply the child portrayed in "Tales" also reflected the voice of a white child, mid-century, in a white suburb of a city in the northern Midwest, a child surrounded by images in magazines, in books, in school, and on TV, that were almost entirely white and obsessed with manifest-destiny. Those images were so unquestioned in family and community that it was possible for that young child to fetishize a coonskin cap, á la Fess Parker's television portrait of Davy Crockett, and be utterly unaware of Crockett's history as a tracker and killer who participated in a massacre against the Creek Indians in 1813.

How are you, Linda, my ghost?

Dear Sam:

That is a story you have yet to write, Sam. I'm waiting for it. And believe me, it wasn't only the myths of my childhood that kept me writing. In the eighties many of my gay male friends were beginning to die. No one really understood why they were getting sick, but it was clear they were being vilified and ignored. Visibility became even more important. It seemed vital to explore not only the persona of my gender through language, but to write my desire into poems, to declare my reality on the page, and to say what I could not find in the majority of the published work I read. My writing often understood things before I did. I also knew that there were children who felt the way I felt as a child. Part of me needed to write my experience for them.

It was "The Shower" that bothered my family the most. I wrote the piece in the first person, in the voice of a child taking a shower with her father. In the poem, the child experiences things she is frightened by, but does not understand. The perpetrator was not based on any one man in particular, but based on so many. I knew some of them. Some were in my family. Some were my friends' fathers. Some I read about. I experienced something similar to what that child had experienced. Not from a father, but from someone, I cannot remember who. The piece came fast and fully formed out of me onto the page.

The week following its conception, I read "The Shower" to the group gathered in Gloria's apartment. As the words of the poem came out of my mouth, I felt my body get very small, the size of a paperclip. My voice began to sound distant, and suddenly I saw myself sitting in the corner of the room, a tiny speck, while the others in the workshop seemed very far away. I felt that if I kept reading I would be killed. I thought that if I stopped, I would also be killed. I somehow kept on and finished the piece. My hearing had closed down and I could not understand anything anyone was saying. After the workshop, as usual, I managed to walk to the bar with the others. It was a relief, that sear of alcohol down my throat. I kept drinking until my hearing came back.

Dear Linda:

I desperately want you to come back, for you to be the one who gets up and reads the poems in these books. I am holding you. Always. I know that you are a part of me, but today I have a beard.

If this current iteration of me, the beard, the lower voice, the small, trans-masculine me, should give a public reading from *Home in three days. Don't wash.*, a work about sexual obsession, I fear that the poems would take on meanings that were never intended. These were letters written in the voice of a gender-nonconforming woman to a woman, both playing with power through consensual sex, a context where certain liberatory possibilities of sex are available.

It's important to me that your name is prominent on these books, and that your understanding of the world at that time is retained. In so many ways, your writing helped bring me into being. It seems to me that we were in a collaboration then, and continue to be to this day. Taking credit for the books, and publicly declaring them solely the work of Samuel Ace, would be a falsehood.

Dear Sam,

I feel like I am always reassuring you. I was tired of the sweet labia- and flower-filled sex I found in the work of so many lesbian poets in the 1980s and early '90s. I did not see my own life reflected in this work. Instead, I wanted to show sex as I knew and imagined it between two consenting adults—the fumbling, the taking on and off of masks, the confidence and lack of confidence, the power and role-play, the desire, the vulnerability, the humor, the stains, the overwhelming obsession of lust and love. I tried to write about sex that was as messy as it was transcendent, as influenced by the culture as much as it tried to break free.

I was not alone. I was writing *Home in three days. Don't wash.* in an environment of women who wanted to write more explicitly about sex. Jesse Helms was ascendant with his crusade against the NEA 4. The sex wars were raging, pitting the anti-porn feminists against sex positive writers and thinkers. Many of us, including Susie Bright, Amber Hollibaugh, Jewelle Gomez, Patrick Califia, Holly Hughes, Dorothy Alison, Carol Queen, Cheryl Clarke, Tristan Taormino, Annie Sprinkle, Joan Nestle, and others, wrote honestly about women's, and specifically lesbian, sexual experiences. As I saw it, sex was as fit a subject for poems as any other part of life.

Essex Hemphill, Carl Morse, Assotto Saint, and many other gay poets were there too. Once at a reading, when some women walked out after hearing some of my more gender-fluid and sexually explicit poems, they stayed, singing, whistling, and encouraging me not to stop. Later, as they were dying of AIDS, they told me not to give up writing all of it down. I still hear them, my singing ghosts.

Linda was one of the most popular girl names in the fifties. If I had been born a boy, my name was to be Daniel, the name of the child my mother lost by miscarriage before I came into the world. So now I almost rhyme with you. Just slant.

My dear Linda,

Perhaps bringing back these books is a form of restitution, allowing that sweet five-year-old face I found in an old photograph to exist. In that photo, you are so skinny, standing next to your cousins in a loose fitting pink dress. You look as if you had just been crying. Why, I don't know. Maybe it was from the last fight you had with your mother about putting on a dress. You look nothing like Timmy, nothing like anyone but yourself.

Before I say goodnight, I want to tell you how grateful I am to you. I still hold you in my heart, and always will. You alone gave me my name. It too came out of you fully formed, not as Timmy, not as anyone but you. It was your invention, your Jimmy Ace, the Monkey Boy, who *sleeps under the stars where the light is blue and green and there are sometimes wolves but the wolves are his friends   they sing to him Hello Jim Ace across the plains   Hello Jim Ace   my ears have grown larger than monkeys' ears   Hello I shout back across the plains   then the night floats down and the wolves come close and lie in a circle around me   where I am the center and I sleep*

Yours in love,
Sam

NOTES

1 Trace Peterson and TC Tolbert, eds.,
*Troubling the Line: Trans and Genderqueer
Poetry and Poetics* (New York: Nightboat
Books, 2013).

2 Anzaldúa, Gloria E. "Speaking Across the
Divide: an email interview," *SAIL: Studies
in American Indian Literatures* 15, nos. 3-4
(Fall 2003-Winter 2004): 17 and 18.

3 Joan Larkin and Elly Bulkin, eds., *Lesbian
Poetry: An Anthology* (Watertown, MA:
Persephone Press, 1981).

4 Barbara Smith, ed., *Home Girls: A
Black Feminist Anthology* (Boston and
Tallahassee: Naiad Press & Kitchen Table:
Women of Color Press, 1983).

5 Gloria Anzaldúa and Cherríe Moraga, eds.,
*This Bridge Called My Back: Writings of
Radical Women of Color* (Boston: Kitchen
Table: Women of Color Press, 1983).

6 Joseph Beam, ed., *In the Life: A Black
Gay Anthology* (New York: Alyson Books,
1986).

7 Joan Larkin and Carl Morse, eds., *Gay and
Lesbian Poetry in Our Time* (New York: St.
Martin's Press, 1988).

The Roads

I wake beneath quilts   sunlight and wind   the
smell of salt from the bay   our child bangs on waves
along the point as our past rolls out from the molting
of poplars   the quiet rust of leaves   the buoys a
secret sign of gospel

The road into the green   the loud green roof of
the B&B at the bottom of the dip and out beyond the
shallows of Chéticamp Island   facing west   I sit
on a chair at the wooden table and stare out at the
yellow house across the way   I've been treacherous
almost fatal   bringing wild grasses into our living
room   my nose a forest   so much hope then so
many birds   the waters   the waters   the god-
sent waters   my tiny shack   heart and bird flown
the afternoon a crescent   the lobster boats arrive in
threes

A havoc of winds along roads that yesterday ran with
frogs   the light a coronation   I give you bearings
for feet and sink my heels into you as we slide into
the corners of rooms   we take our little pieces of
years between our hands to offer a banquet   who
would you invite?   puma or lover?   mother or
thundercloud?   we sit just inside what the herons
call a bowl   we too believe it's a bowl   a tuning
fork   its long note just below what we can hear   it
molds to our collarbones   our ribs and vertebrae
before an echo fills the space between lungs and
throat   I would call a centaur   a horned acrobat off
the Siberian plain   until we fall away to become a
train   a low chime   a hum

We travel a journey of devotions   one's an old man
and one's a garden   another a jeweler who builds
tiny cakes from humid sediments   another winds her
way to Nain through a future of oxbows   a waterfall of
laughter and blood rushing into time without rockets
or ransoms   instead a delicate finity between index
finger and thumb   the refuse that gathers around our
feet   a herd of geese   a few pigeons flown up from

21

the Gowanus and the pier off Red Hook   riding the
old Dutch roads to the abandoned waterfront where
I once watched boys swim on summer afternoons
we will find the cool water they said   and they did

I know a kind of peccary from the southwest   slick
with swamp mud   a pack full of them at dawn
waiting for us to walk outside   instead we jump
through a window into the dark waters and swim
crawl when necessary   eat dirt to tunnel toward the
coast along the map we set out in a New York City
apartment some 30 years ago   where I served you
ice for the sweltering night   now a blanket   a bottle
of water and sparkling lemonade   the faint moon
over your shoulders   the rumble of trains in the hills
begun in the dirt of the east   but long traveled to
arrive at the juncture of these seven clouds   so much
bright air

The plum has a half-life and a renewal   both food
and tree   singing in the night with the skin of the
dark rose   we meet at the tips of new suns   each
an eyepatch   a quiver   a comfort for cool days   a
pile of laundry in the corner   two white socks without
gravity   a black t-shirt   a pair of jeans with yogurt
stains that look like cum   chiming in unison at 4 a.m.
when I bow to watch a ball of baby spiders   their
mother's vigilance   just inside the front door

I look down at the wood floor and wonder who laid
it   wonder where tonight's rain landed at dawn   I
look up at my great grandmother   murdered in the
last century   what did she do with her mornings?
who did she hold?   her cyphers now inside a
Montreal Starbucks where a child's laughter rings out
over a man who steps down from a carriage drawn
by a blinder-blinded horse   I hear him   not the
man but the horse   then the child who now chants
code   a stillness   a blue shirt   an architecture that
summons me to enter the hospital where Nan's heart
stops without her permission   then beats again   a

reminder of how the heart knows itself   her eyes
open to Sonny's smile   when after a pause   she
smiles in return

Yes to trains   between beginning and destination
where I am free to burrow into the unoccupied seat
to my left   to sleep under the sound of wheels and
motors   hidden in the blur of passing fields   two
Februarys ago in Tucson where we find fossils and
meteorites under an ashy tarp   still untouched
by weed killer and car exhaust   I had come for
scrapings but instead heard the clacking mounds of
beads   pearls in heaps   some a flamboyant pink
some a watery lavender   flying off their frail strings
like confetti blown into a cloudy sky   now I sink
further beside the rise of hats and skirts   a chorus
of ancient aunts who arrive daily from the city   they
come to collect minerals   filling their skirts like they
once filled them with child   the fabric bleached a dull
smoke grey by the soil   mud mixed with blood   a
tonic of salt and heat   in the shadow bones I am an
afternoon

Prayer   my friend explains   a way of making breath
before there is no breath   for calling light and
gratitude before the red dirt   so absent from what
we smell for miles on the road to Marfa   shit knee
deep inside the fences where hundreds of cows
stand stunned   as if their bodies were not bodies
their souls not souls   later in the hotel we watch a
video clip of a calf   rejected by its mother   then
raised inside a house by a family of humans   in the
house the calf behaves just like the family dogs   or
perhaps just like a calf   chasing a stick   sleeping
beside the wood stove   licking her humans alive

Now I remember the symptoms   the loud TV in the
upstairs den   my younger sister doing homework
to a cartoon fight on the screen that hides the fury in
the kitchen below   coats like heavy metals   locked
away from the snow   I take them out and find little

doorways of grace   the dirt from my grandmother's
apple tree   a pile of baby mice beneath the woodpile
mewling but safe   until we accidentally disrupt their
home   we agree to put them back   to tuck them
under the old schoolhouse where I now sit in a plastic
chair long abandoned by children   mine a faded blue
others pale green and grey   one red   painted with
a portrait of a girl   a particle left for me to send back
to you   still looking out   until we move   or until
the missiles come   or at least until the night when we
become like the brittle stars that send out a glow and
a foul taste   a warning to the ghost crabs who know
to flee when they encounter such vivid reminders of
a ruinous meal   if you run I will run with you   just tell
me where   I call to the silent air   reach again to find
you   so perched inside another time   our incarnation
breaks the world

Normal

s

e

x

To Gloria Anzaldúa, for the beginnings

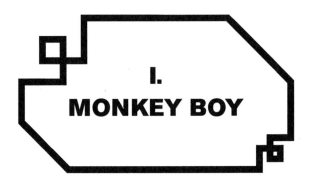

I.
MONKEY BOY

MONKEY BOY

I lift my hand to my face   my hand's the biggest thing around and filled with rivers   it has stems I can see through to the dark fuzzy air   I hold my hand to my face and down below I feel my legs curl up to my chest   I look out at the door of my room it's open a crack and there's light   it's pink and dim   nightlight for Daddy to see when he comes in the crack   light for me not to be afraid   monkey's here too   I can feel his hard face and his big ears and the straps that hold up his checkered pants   his name is Jim and he sleeps with me every night   he's here when I'm naked   he's here when I open my eyes and my stomach hurts and the bed is wet   he's here when I'm high on a pole stuck right up through me and people are laughing and I can't get down   he's here and he runs on his hard curly toes and takes me away like he'll go and get somewhere like Wyoming where I can jump into his body and be there too   in Wyoming my name is Ace   Jim Ace the monkey boy who can run forever and climb the tallest trees   whose hair is dark and whose eyes can see rattlesnakes a mile away who has no mother or father and lives fine by himself Jim Ace the monkey boy sleeps under the stars where the light is blue and green and there are sometimes wolves but the wolves are his friends   they sing to him Hello Jim Ace across the plains   Hello Jim Ace my ears have grown larger than monkeys' ears   Hello I shout back across the plains   then the night floats down and the wolves come close and I lie in a circle around me   where I am the center and I sleep

LIGHT

First there's light then there's dark   in the dark it
doesn't matter if I have my glasses or not   I can see
with my ears   I lie on my back   at first I don't hear
anything   then the ceiling starts to fall   there's a
light with flowers up there   I hang from that light
it's an air light   it's a cracked ball   the air swings
with me   who's that walking?   I hear ice in a glass
it must be Mom   I don't know what she does at
night   she walks back and forth and back and forth
Dad snores on the other side of the wall   I can't go
to sleep   there's a spider flying around in my light
there's a fish coming down to catch me   there's a
train set full of bridges and crashes   there's a planet
and a dinosaur   I crawl up on my knees   I hum
down low   it makes me quiet   I hum louder   the
hum crashes against the train and the dark   I bite
the pillow   my feet run without me   I try to catch
up until there's a door   my dog's on the other side
but I can't get through   I fall on my back in the bed
when I open my eyes the air's not so thick   I can see
the windows and the dresser   the door is open   the
light in the hall is gone

RADIO

She sits with her legs stretched out on top of the
radio   fan blowing up between   a baby reaches up
and out   the bars are high   its face is red   it cries
a something ma-ma-a something ma over and over
the fan muffles the sound but it's there in the room like
a spreading rash   the weather's too hot for anything
let alone a baby   too hot to hear it and smell its puke
no one around to help but the baby's grandfather and
the girls downstairs   too hot to get up and turn off
the Andrews Sisters   her husband's off working and
it's a shame   thought he'd make more of himself
than building houses and coming home smelling like
tar and sawdust   it's a dirty business   and on top
of it all they have to live here   paint chipping off the
ceiling and walls falling down   no other way to afford
a place   her own father on the ground floor running
his bar   or more like he just watches it run   no way
this child's gonna grow up around drunks and freaks
and its grandfather slinking around haunting its heart
the baby's cries get louder   lost three before this
one   shut up   blow on it   soap it down   she
stands   picks up the fan and points it directly on
the baby   walks into the kitchen and comes back
carrying a blue tray of ice   she turns the ice tray over
and watches as the ice cubes bounce off the baby's
head   ice little baby   feel good?   that's real fine
she walks out of the room and slams the door   the
fan drowns out the baby's screams   ice melting
around its ears

HE TOUCHED ME

He touched me and the shivery circle came around my head   he touched me and my eyes went out   out pretty girl   out   he touched me and my belly skin got small   my back skin crawled away   he touched me black hair   he touched me and I couldn't breathe   if I sucked the air the ants would come back to my ribs I'd turn inside out and shrivel up   he crawled down on my belly   what are you?   he reached down to my toes   three little piggies   there was a song in my ears   low auouu like a hundred cows   he touched me and the scent of burning took me up in the air up and I couldn't see anymore   couldn't hear   he touched me and the rush of me rushed out and I got knocked through the air

Mom was at the door   from the ceiling I saw him reach over my head   he closed the Bambi book and put out the light   he lifted up from me and kissed my forehead   good night he said and got up   the bed sprung up to catch me as he went out the door   I sighed and breathed back into myself   I felt lighter than air and the ghost blue nightlight floating in the dark   there was wind outside   I heard it as the cows died in my ears

THE SHOWER

My voice is thin   I stand in the shower   what's that?
I ask   I am at the level of that   what is it?   a penis
he says   men have them   I stand there watching
it   I don't have one   girls don't have one   he holds
it for me   touch it   can I touch it?   long and skin
thick over something hard   thicker than all my fingers
it moves under them   it's not a part of him   does he
take it off when he puts on his clothes?   we are taking
a shower   he is holding it to show me underneath
this is the scrotum he says   like two eggs   what's
all that raised over them?   touch it   veins he says
hairy   he is very black hairy there   I am pink   what
does it do?   it's something men do   my face is no
taller   I am pink and he is hairy black hair   against
the wall are knobs to make the water go hot and cold
my back is against them   he tells me not to be scared
and rubs his fingers through my hair   curly head he
says   it's just the difference between boys and girls
he is not a boy   he is my father   boys are on TV   a
boy is a friend of Lassie and rescues things   boys are
me   smooth like me   he is still showing me   the
shower walls are there   knobs like a gate I can't go
through   I have to stand in the middle   I have to see
him   the water protects me   falling between us like
rain falls   make it hotter I tell him   scared makes
me cold   time to wash he says   no I say   first I'll
wash you then you can wash me he says   no   I
don't want to wash   I want to sit down in the water
the hot makes my heart beat too fast   he has the
washcloth   he is washing me anyway   soaping my
back   the thing hangs down on me as he bends over
to scrub   it's sticking up   brushing back and forth
along my shoulder   I pull away   I'm almost done he
says   stand still and let me wash your legs   I have
to pee   his legs are hairy too   I've seen them before
what's wrong?   he tickles me in the ribs with the
washcloth   it's rough and orange   more will come if
I pull away   my serious little girl   what's wrong?   he

tickles more   I am laughing   no   I try to pull away
be careful or you'll slip   he holds me and tickles me
all over   I can't get past the water or the walls   he
drops the soap   my feet lift off the ground   he holds
me by the shoulder   I laugh and cry   he can't tell
if I am laughing or crying   I am going to pee   he
pokes me in the stomach   he is laughing   that penis
thing shaking as he laughs   had enough?   now let
me wash you   I can't hold it   I am peeing   I bend
down to get the soap to hide that I am peeing   he
doesn't notice   the water runs too hard   I hand him
the soap   I am done peeing   he washes up my legs
feet first   up into my crotch   washing me because
I am dirty   washing the pee away   he washes me a
long time   moving the washcloth and soap back and
forth   I stand on my own   staring at the dark tiles
at the water beading and falling by its own weight   far
away I hear him whistling   he echoes in the walls
OK   you're done he says   it's my turn   I tell him
to turn the water hotter   I'm getting cold   it's not
cold he says   yes it is   he turns the water hotter to
please me   he hands me the washcloth and points to
his stomach   here first he says   I wash his stomach
reaching out and above the thing below   good he
says and pulls me to him   my arms around him   the
thing is in my face   my neck   he tells me to wash
his back   he holds me there   I am choking   I can
barely move my arms   you have to wash harder than
that to get me clean he says   I try to wash harder
his legs are shaking   his knees around my own   I
am choking   I try to say I'm done   he calls down to
me   what?   not letting go   I drop the washcloth
and grab his hips and push away   the thing springs
out after me   following me   I turn away and try to
open the door handle   I can't reach it   I look at him
I'm done I say again   you're done?   but I'm not half
as clean as you he says   I have to go   I'm cold   he
stares at me and says I guess your daddy is just going
to have to get clean himself   there's a towel for you
outside on the rack   be careful and don't slip   he
opens the shower door for me and closes it when I'm

36

outside   I am surprised the rest of the bathroom is
still there   white and steamy   the mirror covered
with fog   I pretend I am hidden in the steam   I pull
the towel to me and hold it to my belly   my belly is
tired from the pee being forced out   I hear my daddy
singing and look through the glass door of the shower
to see his shadow washing himself   he sounds happy
he stops singing   I can see the pink outline of his
hands   not hairy now   washing the thing   penis
he washes and is silent   it must take a long time to
get it clean   then I hear his breath and suddenly he
shouts like he has hurt himself   his breath is fast like
he is getting mad   he will come after me   I made
him turn it up   I throw the towel up over my head and
run out of the room   the water got too hot   I made
him turn it up

II.
TALES OF A LOST BOYHOOD

BALLET (1943)

Sylvia remembered that they had been around forever, living together up on the eleventh floor. Sylvia lived on the second floor, just above her father's bar. Elva, the older one ("that baby of a girl is gonna leave me someday for a younger woman"), baked brownies for her. Elva would tweak her cheek in the hallway near the elevator while Sandy stood there shaking her head, saying, "Always wanted kids, didn't you? C'mon now, Elva, let's go." In the hall, Sandy wore a dress. It looked like a costume on her. Up in their apartment, she wore pants, and that's how Sylvia thought of her: Sandy, the one in the pants.

Elva told Sylvia to come up anytime and she often did, even though she had to be sneaky about it. Her mother didn't like her going up there. "You stay away from those girls," she would say. But Sylvia loved food and Elva's brownies only next to ballet dancers. Up there, Sandy and Elva lived like they were married. Elva would show Sylvia pictures of her mother in Texas, while Sandy, feet up on the sofa, listened to the radio in the living room. Sylvia's mother never let her put her feet on the sofa. Elva would ask Sylvia about school and listen to her talk about ballet. Elva was a better person to talk to than anybody. She never stopped her, never interrupted, never had something else to do.

The pink slippers are on the table. They're brand new and Elva's given them to her. Sylvia can't stop looking at them. "Look, Elva," she says. "Look. Can't you see? I'm up there, up on a stage. My chest is thin and my skirt goes out from me like a pink cloud. Look, my arms are up, stretched so high I can touch the ceiling. No, the sky. Look Elva, there's green behind me painted with deer and swans. My legs are long and thin and my feet are stretched up, up. I'm not touching the floor anymore. Oh Elva, thank you, thank you." Elva comes around the table, hugs her and says, "Have another brownie." Sylvia's already had two, but she takes another and puts it in her mouth. Her skirt is too tight now, but she doesn't care. Elva makes better brownies than her mother. "I'm gonna be a ballet dancer," Sylvia says. "I'll put on these shoes and they'll make me like air and I'll fly."

They hear someone walking down the hall. "It sounds like my baby's finally made it home," Elva says. Something heavy falls on the floor outside the door. "Damn, damn!" they hear. There's another loud bang. Elva gets up and goes to the door. She opens it and says, "Having trouble, honey?" Sandy slams the door open, hitting Elva in the arm. Elva's face gets hard. "Sandy, you been downstairs with Max again?" Max is a girl too. Sylvia's seen her here before, drinking beer and listening to the radio with Sandy and Elva. "I ain't been nowhere," Sandy yells. "So look who's here." She walks over to the table and stares into Sylvia's eyes. "It's Elva's kid. Elva's lousy kid. Always wanted a kid Elva, huh, huh?" Sandy crushes Sylvia's ballet slippers under her elbows.

Suddenly Sandy whirls around and strides across the kitchen to Elva who's still at the door and still looks mad. Sandy grabs Elva's rear end with her hand. "Not in front of the child," Elva yells. Sandy doesn't listen. Laughing, she drags Elva across the kitchen to Sylvia. She sits down in a chair, pulls Elva backwards onto her lap, and holds her arms pinned behind. Sylvia can see Sandy's slicked-back hair and leering smile above Elva's shoulders. "You ever seen a woman before?" Sandy asks Sylvia. "You leave Elva alone," Sylvia screams and gets up. She starts to hit Sandy with her fists, but Sandy laughs and pushes her away hard. Sylvia hits her head against the wall. "I asked you," Sandy says, "you ever seen a woman before?" Sylvia can't answer. Her head hurts and she's crying. Elva's screaming, "You bitch! Let me go---this child---!" Sandy won't let her finish. She holds Elva's arms with one of

40

her hands and rips open her blouse with the other. Elva's got on a brassiere underneath. It's so white that it hurts Sylvia's eyes. Sandy pushes Elva forward and unsnaps the bra. It falls around her shoulders. Sandy jerks Elva back up so she faces Sylvia again. "There," Sandy says, cupping Elva's breast for the girl to see. "Pretty, ain't it?" Sandy pinches the nipple red. Elva is pale. She says, "Sandy stop, please stop." "Come here kid," Sandy demands. Sylvia doesn't move. "See it?" Sandy asks as she pinches the nipple harder. "See what happens? Yours'll stand up too one of these days. Want to try? No?" Sandy pulls Elva's skirt up her legs. She spreads Elva's legs over her lap. Elva doesn't move now. Her underwear is white like Sylvia's. Sandy grabs in between Elva's legs and pulls away the underwear. It's brown and hairy. Elva's making another noise. Elva! Sylvia wants to scream. "You'll be that way too," Sandy's voice rushes across the room. "Just wait." She pushes Elva to the floor. "C'mon, Elva. Let's show her some more." Sandy sits down on Elva. Elva moans and yells to Sylvia: "Take your slippers and get out!" She sounds desperate and mean. Sylvia crawls to the door. She stands up and reaches the knob. She will have to go back past them to get the slippers. "Get out!" Elva screams again. Sylvia's eyes go wide and black as she backs out of the door, leaving her slippers behind.

TALES OF A LOST BOYHOOD

I. Drummer

I dream I'm in a field. There's a dog barking. It's Tammy. She's come to walk with me. The sky carries us up. It's summer in my dreams. Last summer when I was a bare-chested Indian boy and saw the devil's paintbrush.

Paintbrush in the linoleum. I sit on the floor in the kitchen. My mother is making dinner. Dinner smells in the stove and on the roof. The cabinets are high above. The specks in the linoleum are beetles. A swarm of bugs that eat houses. They eat and eat until their eating is a roar and my father walks in the door. He's big. He has on a suit and tie. He's left his car outside even though it's small enough to fit under the table. That's what my mother says. Dad kisses Mom. The dishes in Mom's hands are heavy. She can't let go to kiss him back. Dad walks over to me. "Hello little girl," he says. Hello little boy is what I hear. Suddenly I'm up in the air. My father smells like trucks. The floor is upside down. Bugs crawl up my father's legs and stomach. My sister walks in and my father swings me down into a chair. He pulls my sister up like he did me, only my sister laughs. She likes it. She dances. Mom's lips get thin. "That's enough," she says. "It's dinnertime now."

Everyone's at the table. "What did you do today?" Dad asks Mom. Mom serves the lima beans. There's a table in the middle of a big room. I'm on one side with my sister. The baby's in a high chair on the other side. Mom sits at one end and Dad at the other. "What did you do today?" Dad asks again. Mom's not angry anymore. She cuts up pieces of light brown meat for the baby and tells me to start eating. I have to finish everything on my plate. My plate's not full, but I don't like any of it. I look up and watch my father's face talk and eat at the same time. There's food under his lip. I look down at my plate and push the potato over the meat so it looks like I've eaten something. I do eat a lima bean and that tastes good and clean. Mom tells Dad what she did in school today, that her teacher said her paper was excellent. I think my mother is learning things I'll learn someday. Then I think that's not true. I'm making it up.

I'm really a drummer. I drum most of the day. If I drum, dinner will be over. My mother tells me to stop drumming. If I drum, all dinners will be done and I can take off my skirt. I hit the glasses with my knife. The baby stops eating to listen. I drum better than the man in the orchestra with the big bowls. The glasses bang and bang. Bang. Mom stops talking. She stares at me. My sister looks sad. Dad grabs my hand and the knife knocks over a glass. I try to catch it but I push my plate off the table instead. "Look what you've done! Look what you've—" Mom yells. She swings her arm over the table at me but catches herself before anything happens. My hand freezes around the knife. Mom gets up and walks into the kitchen for paper towels. She won't look at me while she helps me wipe up the mess. I'm not doing it right. I've got my skirt full of milk. Mom tries to clean the baby's tray and the baby throws a piece of potato at her. I slide out the door into the hall and up the blue stairs to my room. I take off my skirt full of milk and leave it on the floor. I find my jeans and put them on.

I walk to the closet. I take down some hangers and rip the ends of the wire parts out of the cardboard tubes. I have real drumsticks now. I play the cardboard tubes on the bedspread so they can't hear downstairs. I play in all the patterns and all the flowers like Harry Belafonte. Sometimes Dad listens to Harry Belafonte. There's a fence in the bedspread. I play in that fence. I bounce over it and there's a stream. I walk in the stream and the trees tower over me. They stand naked for a long time before they reach their full and leafy tops. I throw rocks in the water. One sound is like a bell. The next like my drum. There are frogs too. Green and portly frogs like the hearts of bears. I have on lederhosen and a purple shirt. I walk. One bare knee, then the other. I follow my knees all the way down the stream. I walk with a stick on my shoulder. At the end of the stick there's a red bandana tied around all my belongings. A metal plate. A knife. A flint. A fishing line and a hook. One pair of socks and an extra shoelace. I need very little. I walk with the fish. The stream runs through my head and out my feet. I throw my hair in and out of the water and raise my arms and bring them down again. I hear a rooster and a clap. Someone is coming up the stairs. I hide my sticks under the pillow and run into the bathroom. I turn the water on in the sink and listen. I'm hidden in a waterfall. A one-eyed bandit. The one with the patch and the German Shepherd dog. My dog will tell me when it's safe to come out. Just be quiet and wait, I think. Just be quiet and be.

2. Bug

I'm sure it's there. I can see it. It's bigger than the light bulb, bigger than the whole light. My eyes can't move. If I shout, it will fly into my mouth. I see it spread its wings over the baby's crib. I close my eyes, but then I have to see. It will fall on me if I don't see. There. Now it's in the far corner away from the door, away from the bed. It's my chance. I have to get out of bed and I do. I slide along the wall, keeping my eyes glued to its body. I don't have on a pajama top and my chest is cold. Now it's crawling toward me. Go, I tell myself. It's coming. Go! My arm is barely long enough to reach the door. I have to run now or the bug will fall on me. I open the door and I'm out. I slam the door behind me.

"Grandpa!" I yell. Grandpa is baby-sitting tonight. It's quiet downstairs. "Grandpa!" I scream again. Grandpa comes to the foot of the stairs. He's so little, the bug will kill him. Then it will eat his arms. Grandpa walks up the stairs and opens the door to my room. He switches on the light and looks. The back of Grandpa's head is square. "I don't see anything," he says. I look in under Grandpa's arm. The room is pink and the baby is still sleeping. "It's in the light," I yell. "You have to get it." Grandpa looks down on me. "It's in the light!" I yell. Grandpa goes to the basement for a ladder. When he comes back we walk into the room together. I watch from my bed while Grandpa climbs up toward the ceiling. Now the bug will get him not me. Grandpa looks into the light. "It's not here," he says. I don't believe him. I tell him to take off the shade. He does, but nothing is there. It has to be hiding. I look around the pink ceiling but don't see anything. Grandpa puts the shade back on the light, climbs down, and folds up the ladder. He takes the ladder out into the hall and turns off the light in my room. "Leave the light!" I shout. Grandpa turns the light back on and closes the door. I lie on my bed in the light and watch the ceiling. It's in the corner, in the paint, I think. It will jump in my mouth as soon as I close my eyes.

"Shh," Grandpa says. "Shh." He's back. We're in the same place. I'm lying in bed, and the baby is asleep in her crib. Grandpa walks over to twist the music on above her head. The birds go round and round. He stoops down and pulls the covers over her and stands at the crib a long time. She's a baby and I'm her older brother, I think. I sleep in a real bed. The music runs out and Grandpa twists it on again. He comes over to my bed and sits down. He pulls the covers up under my chin. I close my eyes tight. Grandpa pats my head and puts my stuffed dog in my hands. It's a teddy dog. "OK?" Grandpa asks. He tickles my stomach through the covers. "OK?" Something smells like socks. Grandpa's feet are off the floor and on the bed. The bed folds up and I fall inside. I can feel Grandpa's knees inside my ears. My head is cold. I try to push Grandpa away but I can't move my arms. Teddy dog is buried in my side. Something hard falls on my cheek. It's Grandpa's belt buckle. I don't cry. I'm afraid the baby will hear and wake up. Grandpa thinks I'm a girl. My feet want to kick but the covers hold them down. I squeeze my eyes so tight that one of them pops right out of the bed up to the ceiling. It bounces when it hits. The ceiling is pretty up this close, I think, and down there everything is crawling. Grandpa says I look like my mother. My other eye stays on the pillow. It can see Grandpa's white shirt. I come up into Grandpa's chest.

The music stops and the bed fills with water. There's hardly room to breathe. It touches my nightgown. Grandpa leans on the wall. Something tries to get into my teeth. Grandpa's knees slide down my arms. I try to breathe through my nose but it's all stuffed up. Grandpa pushes down. The bed will eat us up, I think. I'm dead now like my dog is dead. The baby screams and the wall falls back the other way. Grandpa's all curled up and sitting on my legs. I can smell him. I don't cry. Grandpa gets up and tiptoes over to the crib. "Shh, baby," Grandpa says. "Shh." He twists the music on again. The baby *shhs*. The birds go flying around. Grandpa comes back and his mouth says good night. He walks out of the room. My eye sees the belt and its buckle lying near my pillow. I push the belt on the floor and pull the covers up over my head. I make a hole for air and twist myself up inside. One of my eyes stays on the ceiling. It watches the door so I can go to sleep.

3. Bath

"Will you wake up?" Mom shouts. I don't want to, but now I'm standing. My pajamas are wet. Mom throws the blankets off the bed and tears away the sheets. They smell. "Are you going to help me?" she asks. I begin to take off the rubber mattress cover. I see yellow drops of pee. "Don't let it drip," she says. I have to pee again. "Young lady," Mom says, "I don't know what I'm going to do with you. This is the third time this week. You're going to have to wash your own sheets." Mom's face is hard and clean. She smells like lipstick.

I leave my pajamas on the floor of the bathroom. My mother has already turned on the bath. I look down at myself and pretend that my penis is hidden by the curve of my stomach. There are two little nipples on my chest. I lift one leg over the bathtub, then follow with my whole body. I talk to myself under the sound of the water. I open my mouth wide. Awoo, I hum. Awoo. I look down at my hands. They're wrinkled from the water, the hands of a potato man, I think, heavy with work. Awoo. Heavy with hearing cows. At first my body looks small and pink. My belly button goes in, not out. My hands are like teacups. Then I close my eyes. Now my body is the potato man's body. Round and squat, skin like burlap and dirt. All day I pick up potatoes and put them in bags. I count: one potato two potato three potato four. My hair is stumpy and my heart is green and black with eyes. It's the large sweet heart of monkeys and potatoes. And it's the eyes that count, one potato two potato three. The eyes that grow, three potato four, the eyes that see.

4. Squirrelhorse

Sit in the corner. That's what I do. The blocks are my house. The house is my boat. Mrs. Donnelly has her hands on her hips. She leans over to say no. "No." A boy looks like he's crying. His tears are on the floor and the floor is dusty in the sun. The paint is drying where we made rivers. There are chickens in my yard. The day just ended and the pigs are in bed. I look up. There's light in the windows and on the ceiling. I fly there sometimes with Peter Pan and dive down. Dive here where my house is a boat and there's a river for it on the wall. Mrs. Donnelly is tall above me. She came when I wasn't looking. "Time to get up," she says. "Time to make butter." I have to come turn the long stick. She takes me over to where the rest of the class has been playing. "OK," she says, "Billy, you get the cream. This is called a churn." We put the cream in the churn. "And you turn like this." Mrs. Donnelly moves my arms around and around. She lets go and it's very heavy, but I turn until my arms are tired. Then Mrs. Donnelly makes someone else take the stick. I walk to the back where I wait a long time. Mrs. Donnelly tells Paige to lay out the crackers. Paige does it so neat. Her mother must make her set the table too. The butter is white. Mrs. Donnelly takes a knife and spreads the butter from the churn onto the crackers. Everyone gets one. I eat and the butter makes a star in my throat. It's cool going down. "What does it smell like?" Mrs. Donnelly asks. It smells like a farm, I think. A farm smells clean like water.

Then we have to go outside. I stand on the steps and look down. My heart starts beating fast and my eyes see everyone in the yard get small. I float up to the sky. The sun comes into me. Everyone looks like squirrels and cats and I am flying. I think to wave but they don't see. The sun is in my toes. It's in Billy's red jacket and Martha's blue ball. I can't remember how to get down.

The siren. Just like Mrs. Donnelly said would happen. It circles around and around on the roof of the school, first loud then soft then loud again. She's showing us how to spell *weight*. She tells us that it sounds like *wate* or *wait*, that the *ie* is a long *a*, like *mane*. A horse's mane and the *a* in *baby* and *wail*. The siren finishes the sentence for her. We knew it was coming. She said it would happen sometime today. We know what to do, but the room is silent. We stare at her and she is silent too. Then she nods her head and we begin to move. The chair at my back is attached to my desk. I slip under the desk and squat on my knees, my forehead resting on top of my left hand on the wooden chair seat. I place my right hand on top of my head so the ceiling won't hurt me if it falls. It's warm and black between my arm and the seat and my closed eyes. The chair is slightly moist. I think I can smell my bottom. I hear Michael's heavy breathing in the back. At the desk next to me, Martha can't get comfortable. The siren goes round and round like an eagle in the sky.

I dream. The eagle picks me up off the ground. I'm afraid to go so high but the eagle won't drop me. Michael snorts and I slide back into my chair. I don't know where I am. My elbow hurts and my head seems too heavy. The siren takes me to a birthday party. All the girls there speak a language I can't understand. It goes *aiaiaiaiaiaiai ah aha*. The girls laugh and wrestle. I sit at the table all dressed up, waiting for the birthday cake to come. One of the girls walks over and speaks to me. She has a dark face and dark hair. She knows I don't understand her and she thinks it's funny. My cheeks turn hot and the color of my red dress. My rear end sticks up in the air. Will she see it? My legs start to hurt. There's a knocking on the wall. A bed creaks and there's more laughter. I try to cover my ears. I hear a sound like the sea, but I can't stay on my knees at the same time. I begin to fall over and catch myself. I open my eyes a little. Martha is still there. Her eyes are closed and the siren continues to circle the room. My arms feel cold. I wonder what Mrs. Donnelly is doing. I think of Lila at home now, washing the sheets. Maybe she's listening to the radio and doesn't know the bombs are falling. She says the sounds of the radio stick to her insides and make her warm. Maybe Mrs. Donnelly is walking around to see if we are holding our heads right. Maybe she can see up my dress.

If I were a squirrel, I could get out of here. No bombs would fall on me. My paws would only look like paws. They would only seem to touch the sky, but really they reach through the clouds and I fly after them to a high field where I open my nostrils as far as they can go in every direction. Like a horse. A squirrelhorse. A squirrelhorse can smell the bombs. Bombs are always full of things that smell, things that spill out of them like rain falls out of the sky. Sometimes they smell sweet like honey or jam. Sometimes they smell sour like throw-up. I catch all of the bombs before they fall. Everyone claps for me. Mrs. Donnelly is clapping. The last siren echoes off the house across the street. It's ending. I want to stay for a while, looking down from my field. The grass is square and green like my backyard.

I open my eyes and crawl out from under my desk. Mrs. Donnelly tells us to be careful not to hurt our backs. Her eyes are red and she stands at the blackboard with her pointer. "W-e-i, w-a-i, w-e-i," she chants. I wonder why she is singing. It's a language I don't understand.

5. Opera

The bus brings me up the driveway. I jump to hit the ground. I'm home. The screen door is too high, but Lila opens it up for me. "You're late today child," she says. "Did the bus drop you off last?" I don't hear her. I'm still in the sky. "Not talking today? OK. Your lunch is getting cold. You go sit right down and eat it." I'm full with butter and crackers, but Lila puts yellow noodles on my plate. She is saying something about the opera. My family is going to see *Aida* next week. It's an Egypt opera. "Girl, listen to me. You got cobwebs in your ears?" I look at how Lila's arms shake in her polka-dot dress. Her hair sticks straight up out of her head. Mine almost does that too. "Wake up!" Lila yells. She gets up and goes to the sink. I take a bite of yellow noodles. Lila is saying something else but I can't hear. "No one ever dies," Lila says. That wakes me up. Now I pay attention. "No one ever dies in the opera. All they do is get up and fall down, get up and fall down. Up down, up down."

Now Lila is on the floor like she's dead. Then she raises up her body and moans. She falls again all sprawled out. I start to laugh. Lila is laughing too. She's up again and crying and singing. My stomach hurts from laughing. "Stop!" I shout. "It never stops," Lila says. "The curtains just got to come down and cut it off." She cries and falls again, then, breathing hard, props herself up on her elbows. "C'mon over here, girl." She motions for me to come. I stop laughing. I don't want to move. "Get over here!" Lila shouts. She lies on her back and sings again. I stand and walk over to her.

Her body looks huge. Lila slaps the linoleum hard. "Here!" she shouts again in the midst of her singing. I lie down beside her. Next to me she is a mountain. "Mark my words," Lila says, catching her breath, "Them ladies always got some kind a life left in 'em." A loud screech follows from her chest. "Heyey!" I feel her vibrate. "Sing!" she calls. I open my mouth. A small sound comes out. I want to tell her that I don't know how. Lila hits me in the arm. More sound comes. I kick my feet. "Louder!" Lila shouts. My voice rises to match hers. Lila grabs my hand and I sit up. We sing long notes into the orange walls. "Heyey, Heyah!" We lie back and sing to the ceiling. I can't tell my voice from hers. We are two opera ladies who never die. Singing like crying, tears fall into my ears. I sing through the walls, my chest as big as Lila's. "Aha!" A loving "ha!" comes out of me so loudly that I laugh again. Lila laughs too. Then suddenly she stops her song. I carry on for a moment, my voice thin and weak without hers. Then I stop too, and we both lie quiet, listening to the air, still and heavy with our breath.

6. Psychiatrist

I wait with Mom in a room filled with couches and *Weekly Readers.* I try to look at one of the magazines and watch the only other person in the room, a woman, when she isn't watching me. The woman looks worried and writes things in a little red book. A boy dressed in a white shirt comes out of the closed door at the other end of the room. He walks over to the woman and she hugs him. The nurse calls out my name. I look up at my mother. She nods toward the open door. I walk into the doctor's office alone.

The room is filled with toys. The furniture is all my size. I sit down at a small table and wait. The doctor comes in, dressed in a white coat, his hands full of papers. He sits in a tiny chair across from me, towering over me and everything else in the room. He has no hair except around his ears. He smiles and says hello, putting the papers down on the table. I say hello back, trying to make my voice sound loud. "My name is Doctor Boz," the doctor says. He reaches over, pats me on the shoulder and tells me not to worry.

Doctor Boz asks me who my friends are in school. I try to think of the girls in my class. "There's Martha and Tina and…" I can't think of any more so I make one up. "Sally," I say loudly. "What's your teacher's name?" asks Doctor Boz. "Mrs. Donnelly," I answer. "Do you like your teacher?" the doctor asks. I don't know but say yes in a quiet voice. I think of the mice she showed us at the science fair. "What games do you like to play?" I feel my heart tighten. Maybe I should have made up an answer before I came.

"Um, tag and baseball," I say quickly. "And hide-and-go-seek." The doctor writes something down on his papers and I wonder if I've given something away. I remember that the mice at the science fair lived in a flat box with wire on top and little walls that formed pathways inside.

"What do you like to watch on TV?" asks Doctor Boz. All I can think of is "Zorro" and "Leave It to Beaver," then I remember Sunday nights and Walt Disney. "Walt Disney," I say. "And I've seen movies too." I surprise myself, offering information without being asked. I think it might make me seem smart. "What movies?" *"Bambi,"* I answer. "And, and…" My mind goes blank and then comes back. "And *Cinderella* and *Sleeping Beauty*." I remember mice running through the box to get their food. Doctor Boz asks me if I remember the story of *Sleeping Beauty.* I see the doctor's face look serious and calm. It reminds me of Dad who asks questions like this every night at dinner. I nod. "Tell me the story," says Doctor Boz. I feel my face and throat itch. I'm sorry I ever said anything about movies, but I start to talk. "There was a baby born and a witch put a spell on her." "Do you remember the witch's name?" Doctor Boz asks. "Maleficent," I say. I know. The doctor will think I'm OK. "Then what happened?" I can't remember. All I can see is a picture of Maleficent in a book at home. She looks very mean and angry and she's dressed in a dark cloak. Her arms are raised like a huge bat and she screams at a room full of people all smaller than she is. I skip the whole story and blurt out: "Sleeping Beauty fell into a long sleep and a prince came riding on a horse and found her castle covered in weeds and he kissed her and she woke up." Doctor Boz looks at me and nods his head. He writes again on his papers. Every time the mice at the science fair ran the wrong way, they would suddenly crouch and freeze. I could see them shaking.

"Do you know what you want to be when you grow up?" asks Doctor Boz. I try to look like I'm thinking. Mrs. Donnelly said the mice shook because they got a little shock of electricity and that was the way they learned to find their food faster. An explorer, a sailor, I hear in my head. I see Bambi running through the woods. "I don't know yet," I say out loud. "Maybe a doctor." The doctor across from me smiles. "That's a good thing to think about," the doctor says and pats my head.

He asks me to choose a toy in the room to play with. I look around. The trucks and baseball bat draw me with some power of their own. No, I think. I can't give away any more about myself. I feel the tea set and the baby dolls watching me. I breathe faster and don't know where to go. Doctor Boz is looking at his papers. My eyes rest on large wooden dollhouse standing on the floor near the far wall. I walk over to it and look down through the roofless ceiling. I feel the doctor's eyes on my back. The house is filled with carved wooden dolls, their shapes thick and barely recognizable. There's a big shape for the father, another for the mother, and small shapes for the children dolls. I can't tell which are boys and which are girls. Trying to ignore my shaking arms, I sit down and pretend to play, lifting each form out and above square wooden rooms.

7. Sister

"She's my sister." I'm saying it as I wake up. It's morning. Seems late. I hear Dad's car drive out the driveway. It's Saturday but he's going to work anyway. Sandra's awake too. There's no school. The day is good. I put on my jeans and my button-down shirt.

We have to get our own breakfast. Mom's not up yet. I push a chair over to the counter, stand on it and take the cereal out of the cabinet. Dad's already made the orange juice. We sit down on chairs with orange cushions that match the orange walls. "Pass the milk, dear," Sandra says. She's playing like we're in a castle. It's after Sleeping Beauty has been kissed by the prince and they're living happily ever after. Sandra still has on her robe and her face is very round above it. Her pigtails hang down past her shoulders. I don't think Sandra looks like Sleeping Beauty but I go along with it anyway. "Cream puffs," Sandra says. "Mmm. Cream and honey." She takes a bite of the cereal.

"Prince, could you tell the servants to get my horse ready?" Sandra asks. "Yes," I say. I get up from the table and walk out of the room as if I'm telling them. I feel tall in my jeans. We'll spend the morning hunting. I come back. "It's done as you wish." I try to make my voice sound low. I put my hand on my hair as if to brush back my bangs. It's knotted up there. Suddenly I remember who I am and pour milk on my cereal. Sandra takes a spoonful of sugar and places the whole thing daintily in her mouth. "The ball last night was marvelous," Sandra says as she swallows the sugar. I'm not so sure. I don't like balls and long dresses. Then I remember I'm the prince, and the ball doesn't seem so bad. I can see my legs in black tights. On top I have on a white shirt. I wear a pendant around my neck. Sleeping Beauty rests on my arm. "Would you like to go hunting today?" I ask Sandra/Beauty. "Yuck." She's Sandra again. "You can't kill animals. That's disgusting." My black horse racing through the fields is now a TV picture too small for me to see. I don't tell Sandra that I was going to bring meat home for her and our young son, Peter. Our son who would be the next king. I eat another bite of cereal. "Your hair's messy," Sandra says. "Mom's gonna kill you." She is not," I say back. "She's not even up." I can't eat any more cereal. I pick up my bowl and walk over to the sink. "Let's go outside," I say. Sandra says I have to tell Mom. We're not allowed outside without telling Mom.

The shades are down and it's dark in Mom's bedroom. In the bed, Mom's hair looks darker than normal. Her closed eyes are puffy. She sleeps hard. I tiptoe close. "Mom." She doesn't hear. "Mom!" I reach out. I don't know how to put my hand down. I allow the tips of my fingers to touch my mother's nightgown. The material slips against her shoulder. I can feel her breathing. I press harder. "Mom, Sandra and I are going out." Mom turns her shoulder without opening her eyes and says something I can't understand. "We're going outside," I say again. Mom nods her head slowly. We've gotten permission. Relieved, I back away quietly. Mom turns over in the bed and buries her head under the pillow. I tiptoe quickly out the door.

"I'm Gretel," Sandra says. She wants the best girl part again. Lizzie and Lauren and Deborah are there too, in the backyard. I don't know which part to take. "Hansel," I say, but Lizzie wants Hansel too. Sandra says Lizzie should play Hansel because she has short, curly blonde hair. "You have to be the father," Sandra tells me. I don't care. Lauren's the witch. It's the right part for her. She's always mean or lying about something and the witch is just what she deserves. Deborah's too nice to play the evil stepmother, so we make up a part and have her play the real mother instead.

First, everybody's inside the house. Deborah and I are together. Deborah's the one I like the most anyway. She lives next door and her mother is sick. She doesn't have any sisters and she takes care of her father who has greasy hair. Deborah and I hold hands while our children, Hansel and Gretel, go off into the woods. Then there is nothing for us to do. "Make noises," Sandra says. So we make noises to scare everyone on the trail in the dark woods. I hoot like an owl. Deborah is quiet and shy about making noises, and her quiet makes me louder. Deborah begins to make little peeping sounds like birds. Then she hisses. It's a snake. She seems proud to have made that sound. I want to hug her. Lizzie and Sandra sprinkle cut grass behind them for a trail. When they come to the gingerbread house, Sandra wants to eat it all up. She calls to Lauren who's supposed to come out now. But suddenly Lauren doesn't want to play the witch. She starts to whine that she has to go home. She makes me sick. I say that I'll play the witch, and I grab Sandra and Lizzie. I feel like they'll do anything I want them to do. I push them down on the ground. "Don't hurt us," Sandra says seriously. She's really scared of me. Her fear makes me feel good. I force them to stand up in a large cardboard washing machine box. "Now my sweet things. Let's cook some dinner." I bring over a pile of mud and grass. They pretend to eat it. I say, "Eat more," and laugh "HAHAHA" real evil. Hansel and Gretel have to eat more and more and get fat. "Let me feel your thumbs," I say. "Are they big enough yet?" I pull hard on Hansel's and Gretel's thumbs. Lizzie and Sandra shout at me to stop, but I don't. I see Deborah watching. She looks like she really believes what I'm doing. I feel my face turn red and I drop Hansel's and Gretel's thumbs. "C'mon. Play!" Sandra says. "It's time for me to be the father now and rescue you," I tell her. "Who's going to be the witch?" Sandra asks. I say that we have to pretend about the witch now. I walk to the far side of the yard and start to swing my arms. I hum in a low voice. Now I am the woodcutter who follows my children's tracks. My arms are thicker than the trunks of trees and I carry my axe on my shoulder. I will rescue my children whom I love with all my heart. Then I will bring them back to my wife, Deborah, who waits for me patiently by the side of the fire inside our little house.

8. Dolls

I sit on Sandra's bed with my horse and Sandra's dolls. The blonde Tyrolean boy rides his Pinto. I watch as they explore a cave. The Tyrolean boy picks the Norwegian girl up off the ground with a sweep of his arm. They ride off together. The boy's pet wolf follows behind the horse. The wolf protects them everywhere, through rocks and cliffs and the desert. She carries their water around her neck. The boy looks at the girl. They ride far away. Then the girl falls off the horse. "Girls!" I say disdainfully for the Tyrolean boy. I look at the other dolls. There's a Russian girl and an Italian girl, both wearing long skirts and frilly blouses. They can't go out into the desert in those things, I think. I get up and walk into my parents' bedroom to look for a comb.

Reaching high on top of the dresser, I take down Dad's jewelry box. The box is brown and flat. I press the gold button. The box opens and inside I touch the green velvet. All of Dad's treasures are here. Four sets of cufflinks and a coin on a chain. Three silver dollars and a tie clip. I put the tie clip on my shirt. There's no comb. I place the box back up on the dresser and look in Dad's closet. I like the suits. Dad has lots of shoes and shirts too. The closet smells like dust. I also like the ties. I pull down a flowered one and place it around my neck. I walk over to Mom's closet where the mirror is. The door is open. Inside, it's filled with dresses. I close the door. In the mirror, the flowered tie hangs down to my knees. It makes me look like a clown. I take it off. Back in the closet there's a black-and-red tie that's as wide as my stomach. There's also a narrower one that's blue and yellow. I put that one on and take off my glasses. I get as close as I can to the mirror and if I don't turn my head, I can't see my ponytail. It looks like I have a crew cut. I almost look like Dad, but I don't know how to knot the tie. I see the comb on the nightstand. I pick up the comb and draw it through the top of my head. It gets stuck in the rubber band that holds my hair. I pull the comb out and put the tie back in Dad's closet.

The Tyrolean boy jumps off a cliff. I catch him and look into his face. He plays a trumpet. I lift my right fist to my mouth. My left hand plays the valves. I comb the boy's hair to the side. There needs to be more of him, I think. Sandra has a scissors in her desk. "OK, girls," I say, "take off your dresses." I undress the Russian, the Italian, and the Norwegian girl, and hide their dresses behind a pillow on the couch. Their panties look like bathing suits. "Get in line now," I tell them. I make the first cut on the Italian girl. Her hair falls on the bedspread. "There, that's better," I say. I cut bangs, then cut all the way around her head. Her hair sticks up all over. There's a hole where her scalp shows. I stand her up. What will Sandra say? My stomach jumps, then I tell myself she won't see. I'll make the Russian girl's hair a little longer. I cut. It doesn't look as good as I thought it would. The dolls' chests look too skinny. I wish I had shirts for them. I put the Russian girl on the black horse. There. Now the Russian girl has a new name. Her name is Jerry.

I look into one of my drawers. I've been hiding a baby doll there under my sweaters. I cut its hair a long time ago. I bring it to the bed. The other dolls look tiny next to it. The baby doll is the giant's baby and lives in a house with a big cradle. The giant has captured Jerry and his friends, Mike and Peter. The boys have to rock the cradle and feed the baby's large mouth. They pour milk down the baby's throat and it chokes. The boys have no clothes. They are cold. They will escape now on their horses. They crawl out through the cracks underneath the doors.

I hear Mom's car drive up the driveway. There's no place to hide the dolls. Sandra will know they're gone. I throw the scissors into the desk and slam the drawer. I brush the strands of cut hair off the bed and into my hand, and run to the bathroom where I flush the hair down the toilet. I hear the door open downstairs and run back into the room to try to put the dresses on the dolls. I accidentally put the Italian dress on the Russian girl. There's no time to change them. I set the dolls back up on the shelf and race into the bathroom again. I sit on the toilet. I hear the refrigerator open and close. "Practice first, then do your homework," Mom says. Sandra asks if she can have a snack and Mom tells her to take an apple. The refrigerator opens again. Sandra walks up the stairs. "Hello," Mom calls up to me. I don't answer and Mom calls again. "What?" I shout down to her. I don't move from the toilet. "We're home," she says. "What are you doing?" I tell her that I'm going to the bathroom. I take down my pants to make it seem more real. "Did you practice your piano?" she asks. "Yes," I answer. I hear Sandra walk into the room. She takes her violin out of its case. I hear the notes—A, A, D, E, G—as she pulls her bow across the strings to tune them. It's quiet now. In my mind I see her eyes scan the walls of the room. She starts to play a scale. I hold my breath. I don't know whether to get up off the toilet or not. The scale goes up and down. It stops, and the quiet lasts a long time. Then I hear a scream and running feet. The bedroom door slams open into the hall. I stand and pull up my pants. I place my hand on the doorknob. When I open the door I am the Tyrolean boy. There's a Pinto horse waiting to take me into the desert.

9. The Bicycle Parade

I puff out my thin and naked chest and stride outside into the 90-degree heat. I am dressed only in shorts and sneakers and raise my shoulders high in the sun. I am strong and proud. I am a soldier in the hot sun of Africa. I am a boatman high on a mast. I am a rodeo rider and hold a thick rope in my hands. Only my hair, pulled tightly back from my forehead into a long heavy braid, slaps against my back and reminds me of my sex.

I admire the work on my bicycle, decorated for the afternoon bicycle parade. I've wound red, blue, and yellow crêpe paper around every spoke of every wheel and every available piece of frame and handlebar. The bicycle gleams as I tie my favorite mascot, a long thick raccoon tail, Davy Crockett, from the back fender. Then I walk down the almost treeless street, houses so close that I can hear the fights inside my neighbors' kitchens. But today I pay no attention as I walk up a concrete driveway, all glittery in the morning light, to a group of my sister's friends. I greet them as if they were my own, feeling separate and strong in my naked and sun-drenched powers. I admire the handiwork the girls have put into their bicycles, all the time thinking how much better mine looks in comparison. I ask them to come with me and they do, wandering around the neighborhood to where their parents are setting up picnic tables and grills for the late-afternoon barbecue. That will happen after the parade, I think. After I win. I start to run and the girls follow me to a sprinkler which throws great arcs of water and rainbows onto me and them and the sun-parched lawns.

With the temperature rising close to 100 degrees, my sister and I rush into the house for lunch and try to eat the tuna fish sandwiches Mom has made for us. I only manage to nibble tiny bites into my soggy bread. Because of the heat, Mom decides we should have salt tablets before we go back outside. I can barely swallow the pills with my milk. I rush anyway for the door. "Put on your shirt," Mom says, lassoing my hand on the latch. She calls me again as I try to squeeze through the door. I've been caught. "Why?" I ask, stomping my foot. "It's too hot to put on a shirt." "Little girls," Mom says firmly, "do not go outside without their clothes on." "So?" "So, nothing. Go put on your shirt!" "No!" I refuse, remembering my strength, my naked powers of the morning. "Then you're not going out at all, young lady." She says the words calm and clear, emphasizing the last two as if to inform me just exactly what I am. I slam my fist down on the table at the power my mother thinks she has over me and does. I knock over a glass of milk, which rolls off the table and shatters on the floor. Mom chases me through the kitchen, trying to avoid the broken glass and the white pool of milk. Picking a hairbrush off the desk, she backs me into a corner. The hairbrush crashes down on my shoulders and arms as I try to pass through the solid wall like a ghost on TV.

I find myself sobbing and retching on the floor, hands covering my face, my back up against the cool white wall. Mom stoops with her back to me, cleaning up the milk and the pieces of glass. Slowly the memory of my beautiful bicycle, sitting outside without me, surfaces in my mind. I stop crying. I have to ride in the parade. I have to. "OK," I say, making my voice firm. "I'll put on the shirt." I stare at the specks in the linoleum floor. There is no response. "Mom!" I say louder. "I'll put on my shirt!" Mom turns around to face me. I look up, then back down. "It's not enough," Mom says. "I want an apology." "I'm sorry," I mumble, trying to control my voice. I don't think about giving in, but only of my bicycle and the parade and getting out. "What?" Mom asks. "I can't hear you." "I'm SORRY!" I blurt out. Mom points to the floor in front of her. "You've got to clean up this mess." I lift myself off the floor with my arms, feeling weak in my legs. I wonder if she is going to let me go. She watches as I swab up the remains of the milk. "There's more over there," she directs me, and I go over *there*, trying keep down the knot of fury which threatens to explode again in my throat. "Can I go now?" I ask weakly. "OK," Mom says, her face unchanging, "but this can't ever happen again." I nod and leave the kitchen to find a shirt. All I want is to get out of the house.

I catch up with the others, joining my sister and my sister's friends, who had been my morning followers. I can feel their eyes on my swollen face as I stare out at them, making my face hard. I try to sound removed and mean as I say Hi. They ride. Halfway around the first block, I catch sight of my scrawny arms as they dangle out of the sleeveless blouse which covers my chest. I've become a part of them, I think. The girls. I'm not any different. I hear their laughter and see their dainty arms and tiny hands lightly holding onto their handlebars. The rage in the kitchen sweeps back over me. I grip my bicycle tighter. I want to pedal past all of them, to pedal past my thin arms and the laughter and the crowds and the blouse that sticks to my back in the heat. I pedal harder and harder until, hard past bursting, I stop. I wait until the last paraders go by. I look up and down the block. Seeing no one else coming, I rip off my shirt and throw it on the grass. Remounting my bike, I ride on at the back of the line.

For a moment, I am strong and free again. I hold my head up and feel the air cool my chest as I ride steadily through the course. I don't care about anything or anyone. But slowly the heat begins to work on me, sending its waves around and through my body, weakening every circle my feet try to accomplish on the pedals. I see all the people who line the street. A few moments ago they seemed to be cheering me on as if I had been a hero rescued only seconds before being unjustly hanged. Now the crowds jeer and yell. They all seem to be laughing and pointing at me. I close my eyes and try to convince myself that they are not all staring at my thin, now strangely cold and clammy chest. Why did I make my bicycle so bright? I catch sight of a woman smiling at me through her open teeth. The cleft between her large breasts and the white edge of her brassiere show vividly under a low v-neck blouse. I grab the center of my handlebars with my fists and clench my arms tightly over the sides of my chest to hide my small pink nipples. My hair scratches my back. My heart beats too fast. My neck and cheeks are burning off in the sun. The bicycle starts to shake. I try to hold on, blinded by the sweat trickling into my eyes. I have to stop or fall.

I stop. I turn my bicycle around, my ears hot and my legs walking on their own back to where I dropped my shirt. I find it and put it on. Did you see me? I secretly and silently ask as I walk home through the crowds. I am hidden now and safe in my covering. I answer back for myself and all the faces lining the street: No. I didn't see. No one saw.

III.
NORMAL SEX

LAWNS

If you take those green lawns and place them into
your body you might have windows   cars   houses
stubble   flesh   sprinklers and labia   if you place
those green lawns and lovely finished sidewalks and
the cracks we all jumped over right here into your
belly   the earth might fall through the sewer system
and we would walk hand in hand down the streets to
the traffic circle planted in elms to the golf course   to
a world where no one with a family 2.5 kids in each
house could have figured on   from the hard wall of
lights outside the windows   who could have known
all those green lawns made this   a me and a you   to
be together here   a river at our backs   your belly in
my eyes   your legs between my own

And still today could I take you there?   could I buy
the house my parents bought in 1963 for 34,000
dollars?   could I move there with you my lover and
our 3 cats and live wedded?   and what if there were
a child?   what would the houses say?   would I care
and why would I be there anyway?   perhaps to go
into business   run the same business that my father
and grandfather ran and live in the wide open because
everyone has the life I might have   I could uncover
the treasure at the bottom of the tree I planted when I
was 7   I could take your green legs and throw them
in the dirt   the cats might like it   there are plenty
of birds but too many cars   like Faulkner in Oxford
we'd live for life at the site of the crimes   just to be
reminded firsthand   to say the grass   that grass
and the iron gates and the stone steps   the culvert
under the 4th green   to say the whistle that Peter's
family whistled to call him in each evening for dinner
to say a neighborhood where any 7-year-old could
wander far and play as a right and a given   just to
lie down and say   lover   I want to see you in the
postage-stamp backyard   to see you stand in the
screened porch with the green furniture in the deep

summer and the dogs on the other side of the fence and the tetherball set   I want to see you lie on the fertilized grass and flower beds where the backyards are visible all the way down to the Brandons 5 houses away   the trees hang down over   I kiss you in public chase you into the house   take pictures of you on the perfect green lawns of Ohio

NIECE AND NEPHEW

My niece looks around the corner where her only interpretation of me is a man in a hat who hides his eyes because that's exactly who I am   red jacket and lips and the way I place my hands up to my face and rub down my chin

What would life be without translation?

Would it be my nephew?   boy with longbow and crossbow knight   joust boy and target practice boy who knocks down castles and holds an arsenal of plastic guns and boy whose swords are two-handed swords because he says they are so big and heavy they need two men to carry and that's the truth   would it be my niece who won't even consider the possibility of high tops or dungarees and has always been that way   high femme girl whose brother targets the garbage and books and me their aunt where the three of us sit watching 101 Dalmatians concealed in black

MOM'S BEST FRIEND

It's as if you went up into your neighbor's house when you were 15 years old and she was 10 years older and had 2 children and yet she looked at you and said I know you   maybe you were the baby-sitter or maybe you were just your mother's daughter and maybe you had already cut your hair and maybe just maybe she was the woman next door who was your mom's best friend whose eyes really did look into yours   who brushed by and was very official about the touch because at first she was completely capable of passing you by   but maybe you were a little bit bold and maybe she showed you the long narrow hall to the linen closet to the basement to the laundry room and stopped as she looked down into the washing machine when suddenly she turned and you stared at her wanting and you did not say anything and then she looked down again and said into the washing machine   You know I don't   and could not say anything else   you reached out and touched her hand and she drew you close and kissed you   she said I know your mom and you said I know you know my mom   she kissed you again and her son ran down the stairs   she pushed you away and started pulling laundry out of the washing machine   her son said Mom where's my tennis racket?   she answered I don't know   Look in the kitchen closet   she said her words so calmly that the kid went upstairs to look again while her sun-dark hand barely touched yours resting on the white enamel where you both waited as if your entire lives depended on the discovery of a tennis racket lost deep inside a kitchen closet

SIGN

I forgot to tell you about the red sheets my sister bought for us that were incredibly cheap on sale and that we couldn't replace with the blue sheets we wanted because the blue sheets were now full price I forgot to tell you about the reason I wanted to make love last night and instead we had a fight   I forgot to tell you that I came out in sign class   a class of twenty or so under-thirty women and one man all from the teaching professions   all straight from E. Greenbush I forgot to tell you that the week before the teacher asked me do you have children and I snapped my fingers together to say no and slapped my hip to say I had a dog   she made me finger spell our dog's name and then the teacher said bring pictures of your family next week   I forgot to tell you that this week I brought pictures of you and our dog   I showed them to the class and when asked I slapped my hip and gave the sign for dog and pointed to the picture of you and made the sign for love and person which is the sign for love person or lover and some of the students looked at me and were very polite   some even smiled   it was so easy to say husband and children and all I wanted to say was lover and dog so I wondered why after all these years I still had to blush

MARRIED

What changes married lady?   is it the make-up you
wear?   the sudden tight lips?   the window closed
'cause the baby can't catch cold?   boy bodies on the
bed?   where is your mouth my mouth?   the punk
and the spike?   your red and wild hair exchanged
for shopping carts and k-mart bouffant?   what
changes married lady?   where are your cashmere
coats your spandex pants your low-cut shirts?   your
eyes across the room holding mine?   today I see a
smile that says   Look   I have this sudden husband
this sudden baby   this sudden school for my young
daughter   I have this sudden fortune so cavalier in
custom   what changes married lady?   your z-car
and the desperate hugs in the dark?   your finger
in my ear?   what changes just when tomorrow you
could die?   you could you know and tomorrow and
all time would be lost   tomorrow could just be me
and the memory of your sudden red across the room
the touch of your hand at the back of my neck   the
possibility of shock   the light that was ours ever in
the sky through the roof   an aurora rarely on a spring
night

DOG

All I smell is dog and all I know is dog   all I care for
is heart and mouth   all I see is fine soft and head
beneath my nails   fine please and thanks   all I know
is dog   big and lovely   herd of gazelle   through
the brush I see the pond full of concentric and not so
concentric circles for issue and stick   all I know is
pond   now summer and yellow swim and raspberries
off the vine   the back seat of any car far and formal
and the reissue of mud   all I know is god and toe and
stick in one hand   frisbee in the other   thrown so
far I cannot make it out in the grass   all I know is dog
collared and streak in play in come in solid weight on
my lap in absolute confidence and exhaustion from
squirrel chase   all I know is dog   Liv Ullman eyes
sweet like flan

EARTHQUAKE

There was an earthquake in New York and everything on landfill fell into the Hudson River   that included me and my dog and my lover toppling over into the grey water from the 34th floor   that included all ghosts and the rain   that included everyone because it wasn't only landfill but everything to 6th Avenue in the west and everything to 3rd in the east I was in her arms as we fell   my lover that is   not the woman I was married to   here we are forever I thought   as we fall   forever captured on the cover of the *NYTimes Magazine*   smoke and orange dust in the background of a late afternoon   falling off the bed into the Hudson River in my lover's arms   falling farther and farther from each other   my dog falling behind with that ohno look on her face   and the bed just behind all three of us ready to fall right down on our heads

And it was 6th Avenue only for a moment   because the next day were the aftershocks   and then the island of Manhattan was gone completely and the shore rested somewhere in Riverdale and the northern Bronx and then the next day the shore was in New Jersey and then in PA   the country was being eaten away at a rapid pace and the people in Ohio became salt water fishermen and women because all the industry was washed away   except of course the Honda plant in Marysville which was now the main office because Japan was wiped out by a tidal wave   and there I was on the cover the *NYTimes Magazine* which survived because the *NYTimes Magazine* was printed in Idaho   and the woman I was married to was on a business trip to Banff in Alberta so she was safe   but only safe enough to see my picture falling out of our apartment with a lover in my arms   Adulterer she murmured under her breath after the shock of my death subsided   Here I am she thought   stranded in Alberta with the

memory of an adulterer   so the business trip turned
into permanent residence and she framed the picture
from the *NYTimes*

I saw the picture on her dresser when I went to say
goodbye to her on my farewell death trip to all my
close friends and relatives   it could have been her
falling out of the 34th floor with me   that is what she
always thought   her   but there she was in Alberta
after all this time   skiing   would you believe she
took up skiing?   and she had a practice which
specialized in earthquake insurance   You can't have
too much she would counsel people   speaking of
her own experience   Never too much she'd say
My entire apartment fell into the Hudson River   she
never told who fell in with it   but it was good advice
anyway

NOVELS NOVELS NOVELS

At home on a Sunday night I try to write a novel and out comes my dog and out comes the TV and out comes my tweezers and out comes my Triscuits and chips which all have to be gone first   out come the pails out come the sandbox and the lifecycle and the calisthenics out come the shower out come the word processor out come the organization the lists the radio the stare of my dog   oh and out go we for a walk and out comes the stick and out comes the phone and the whisper and the porn and out comes the back page of the *Advocate* and out comes every magazine that came new oh and catalog and out comes the Astroglide and out comes the TV without an antenna and out comes the outcomes of two girls riding a bike down a dirt road and out comes the tweezers again   and out come old friends and happy days and a resumé and a letter and out comes a word about a first girlfriend and out comes pleasure and out comes boredom   oh the toilet out comes the fire needs tending out come desert boots and buying spree and pleasantry   1960 and tree-lined blocks and the mall   in comes the car from outdoors and the cold out comes the pencil out comes forms for my job out comes taxes and books and fingers on the keys out comes the music and the rest slow and every piece of candy in the house

GIRLFRIEND

I have a girlfriend who wants to be someone else
not someone else's lover   but a big broad on a
broad Broadway stage   she wants to sing and stand
up and tell jokes and have everyone love her more
than I can love her onto Broadway   instead she is on
the telephone now because she works sometimes at
home being very competent in her job as a consultant
to an insurance company   yes   she sounds very
professional having a conference call   even though I
know she's still in her pajamas and still warm from our
bed   she sounds yes very competent and I only wish
I could make that path for her when she wakes up
out of sleep into her chair where Madonna's fabulous
makeup artist who used to live in our building is
applying makeup at 5:00 at night from the sheets
where we just got up for my girlfriend to go on stage

I have a girlfriend who wants to be someone else
she wants to be a painter and that's all she can think
about   getting up out of her bed which she got
into at 3:00 a.m. after coming from the studio where
she worked so hard she began to lose consciousness
she lost all sense of what she had in mind when she
started that evening   but it worked and she worked
and the heat was almost enough   although she
did have on heavy boots and she did have on a hat
and she wanted a drink but drank tea instead   and
she has these huge photographs   everything is a
photograph and charcoal and paint   she looks like
a coal miner   she has a giant projector in her mind
and the paint flies onto the canvas and the canvas is
immense and suddenly there are two women there
making love   the paint drips high and you can't tell if
one is a redhead or not or if it's the girl in the bed who
is really next door in bed   it is the greatest painting
she ever painted   this painting in her head at 9:00
p.m. as she is trying to fall asleep because she has to
get up at 5:00 a.m. to walk the dog and go to work

where she teaches children very competently   and
where maybe she's seen as a little crazy and a bit odd
to be a schoolteacher in the rural county where she
lives

I have a girlfriend who wants to be a writer well known
in all the right circles and gets up and does 103
readings and performances of her work a year   I
have a girlfriend who is good at everything she does
but wants to be a writer so sometimes she sits at the
typewriter like Jack Nicholson in *The Shining* and
writes *I am a good boy I am a good boy* over and over
and sometimes she finds a break in the fence of good
boys and runs out   her fingers on the typewriter
keys like piano keys   like playing Chopin or Liszt
or Tchaikovsky   and she writes about the bad girls
and good women who populate her breakfast table
every morning   she also works at night because
the day is too bright too sudden and particular   she
writes too as she dresses for dinner with her family
who she smiles at now and patiently waits for as her
father asks about the typesetting and editing business
she also runs very competently and where she edits
science books for children and designs newsletters
for corporate clients who appreciate her "clarity of
style and design" and her "thoroughness of research"

BEETHOVEN

I see Beethoven in the bathtub and he's hidden in the
sound of water   Beethoven is also birds   I heard
that yesterday in the trees   I heard Chopin too and
then the Fifth Symphony   oh sweet singer   what
could it be that you hear?   do you regularly earn the
money to pay for your next sonata?   who will sign
when the water is so high?   like Beethoven   she
became the most famous writer of all time   and
how?   by howling   adoration crept through her
feet like burning coals and she was lowered down
craving pain and craving rescue   on other days she
dreamt of New Mexico   she was that painter living
off the sky alone through noons past and a rooster
raising her arms   a farm of grasslands and plates
with no horizon   it could have been Captain Doom
this time who carried off the world   or it could have
just been an unreachable mosquito bite   she once
wrote that most famous novel and earned all the
money she needed for the rest of her life   so across
the face of her words it was finally OK to ask where
the little Beethoven kept himself   there he goes

LOVER

She carries the garden tools to the hill and starts to
beat a hole   she finds a garland of roses full of ears
and salvage   a shield bush   a crown of peas and
a glass of juice   she has to drink that first   crown
the girl!   crown the two of us   heart and right arm
hair and toe   lip and anus   a chord trembles light
from belly to belly   it shakes in the wind but can't be
broken   oh girl   I choose you   see?   it is ours to
step forward   ours to heal the run of the wheel   a
simple sound   a coo   a clavichord   ear to breast
ear to field and sleep

MUD WRESTLERS

Naked   we are mud wrestlers   leather and wet on
strong forearms in the early morning tide fields   I
stand scraggly in the flats like a strand of marsh grass
mud seals my body from the sun   legs gaunt and
sunk   I run to keep warm   my followers with me
and you   my enemy   form your ranks across the
fields   you dance and prepare   slap green mud
onto pink skins lighting through like painted roses
we shout and carve our power into our arms and
bellies and the mud beneath our feet as if we were
signs sucked out by the loose water of the pounding
tides   we watch each other gather on either side and
wait to cross the distance

I lead and know the strong women behind me will
follow   my thighs buoyed by recklessness   toward
you   a version of me   your warriors following
you   fanning out behind like wild geese become
naked women crawling to meet across the mud flats
of tidal Maine   inhabited only by us and flocks of
jealous seagulls and the great blue herons who bark
out welcome to the tiny life of shrimp and mussels
where the ocean holds its intimate beginnings among
the grasses and periodic waters   here we march   a
taut rope of light draws us unbroken to each other
two ships or rockets destined to collide   the whites
of your eyes shine out to me under heavy brows of
mud   a flicker of a smile plays at your lips   I drive
forward and do not laugh at what began as a game
my face carries through this performance as if it were
real   and you are willing to follow

The others stop but for us this is combat   I throw
myself into you   scratch for your skin under the
mud which opens before me like the pale mouth of
spring   I am driven to devour that skin but my fingers
are unable to grasp anywhere or to hold any part of
you   you try to hold me in the same way and we

slide over each other while the others crouch back to
watch   a sliver of cold shakes me   I am below you
now   the blue sky rises above   clear and empty
of mud   my nose and mouth suffocate as I sink
beneath the weight of you   but I look past you to
those who followed me here and a dense pride takes
hold of me   forcing me up into your belly   my legs
between your slick thighs   my arms around your
neck   slowly I turn you over   burrowing on top of
you now   my cunt and legs spread across yours
my nose flattened against your neck   I crawl frog like
and up to catch you beneath your armpits   I grasp
your hair which hangs over me   long and grainy
through the wet   my other hand slips down to the
crack of your ass   full with mud   pubic hair to pubic
hair   a necessary friction which holds us   when
suddenly I see your eyes go dark and look past me to
the sky   to the old abandoned railroad bridge across
the flats   I feel the fight leave your arms and you
speak for the first time out here   a whisper   *There
are people watching*   I hold your arms pinned to
the mud and look up to see five clammers standing
on the bridge   they point and laugh   sounds we
cannot hear but know   and I know to crawl off of you
thrown into pantomime   mud covers our nakedness
now as we shake in the cold morning of late-August
Maine   forced to bathe ourselves in the frozen tidal
waters to gain back the warming sun   forced to
expose ourselves to the laughing clammers   so high
on the bridge in the low marsh

PASTORAL AND SEA SONG AND FAIRY TALE

Ally at our home in the country   Ally dancing in the trees and fields in her red ballerina dress and her white tights   I am sure she will find animals and fairies when we get up in the morning   a very sunny morning in the south-facing window-filled house Ally and I might take an early morning walk   she will show me the hollow tree where her unicorn Zip lives and where he waits for her to visit   inside the tree is an old nest where cardinals once slept   that is what Ally tells me

> *We will walk back and my lover and my sister, who is Ally's mother, will have made breakfast. There is coffee on the table and plates are set for all of us. Ally's baby brother will crawl around the floor and play with the cats.*

Now back in the city Ally dances into the room   she is dressed in a white petticoat pulled over red tights and undershirt and she carries two scarves   one blue and one green   she twirls so that the petticoat stands out from her body as she raises her arms above her head

> *"Look at you Ally," my lover exclaims. My sister tells us that the petticoat was a gift from a friend who only has boy-children and who loves to give Ally frilly clothes. Even at Ally's age, I could never bear such clothes. I wonder if the love of petticoats is a genetic trait.*

I need music! Ally calls   a record comes on Tchaikovsky   I'll dance with you Ally I say   It's the spring! Ally announces as she dances little spring steps   I join her dancing through the young green plants   I tell Ally everything I see   the clump of

purple tulips and the five robins with their nests of
blue eggs   Ally dances wildly   trailing her scarf
behind   I'm having a wonderful time! she shouts
the music speeds up and crescendos   tambourines
crash   Jump! Ally I shout   Leap!   I fly across
the room   Ally follows   we dance around the old
entrance hall rug   Ally suddenly stops and points out
the window   What's that out there?

*I look across the room. My lover and my sister sit
talking at the table in this, my sister's apartment.
It is a table I know well—the old family dining
room table, rounded at the corners, seats with
wide pads, solid and somewhat modern. In the
home I share with my lover there is very little of
my family's past: a teacup of my grandmother's,
a chipped vase, a menorah, a dusty prayer
book. But here, every corner is filled with
objects I grew up with, transplanted from the
Midwest to these rooms on the upper west side
of Manhattan. Hanging from the round-headed,
long-stemmed chrome floor lamp is a matte-
black mobile of dots and triangles, a gift once
given to our father as a birthday present. A huge
rubber plant stands in the corner. My sister has
been growing the plant since she was a child in
her red bedrooms. My sister always wanted her
bedrooms to look like rooms from* Gone With
the Wind—*red bedspread, red curtains, red
pillows. She insisted once on a red velvet-like
shower curtain in the bathroom.*

What's that out there? Ally asks again   What is it? I
ask back   Why it's a whale in the distance Ally says
definitely   You're right Ally   I agree   It *is* a whale
Ally gets down on her belly   I do the same and we
swim toward the huge beast in the sea   I see a
whale in the distance! Ally calls out again   finally we
arrive at the whale's side   I ask if it is friendly   Ally
says Yes   It is friendly   I suggest we swim inside
the whale   we crawl through the whale's huge teeth

down to its stomach where we meet a man who takes care of the whale's insides   Ally gets bored   she jumps up and runs around the rug   we ride camels to an oasis   Ally likes saying the word   oasis   she finds a stream to drink from because we have not had water for 39 days   the music now sounds slow and sonorous   Ally wants to be a turtle   the birds are singing   Ally gets up and starts to twirl   she loves the way it feels to get dizzy   she closes her eyes and spins until she falls   I'm getting sleepy she says Very sleepy

My lover's eyes travel over the room as she talks. Does she see a past here? I wonder. Have I told her anything about these white, now yellowed couches? Exactly how they sat in the living rooms of my childhood? I see myself at night—a night in my teens. My mother sits reading a large art book across from me. It is late. My mother stops turning pages to look at a painting and takes a sip of scotch from the glass at her right. For a moment, on the couch, a sense of safety and peace surrounds me. It is as if everything had always been, and would always be, all right. The furniture is bathed in light.

Ally wants to play like she is Sleeping Beauty   she raises her hand to her mouth in a mock yawn   the music is quiet   violins play   I'm so sleepy Ally repeats   I have to go to sleep and you have to come and wake me up   I understand what is expected of me   Ally creates a perfectly smooth square out of her blue scarf and lies down on it   she holds herself very still

I tell Ally this story: You are the princess who has been asleep for a hundred years   You are the most beautiful princess in the world   in a universe of princesses   The prince has come from very far away in search of you   He has searched everywhere   in

Egypt   in New Zealand   in Indiana   He has finally come here to this castle which is a very old castle covered in vines and trees   He knows this must be the place and hacks through the vines and trees with his sword to open the gate   The gate squeaks loudly as it opens   Ally's eyes stay closed as I speak   her expression is one of sleep and does not change   I continue   All the people in the castle are asleep They sleep in their chairs   at their counters and stoves   exactly as they were a hundred years ago All the animals are asleep too   the dogs and the cats the goats   the mice   the pet birds   Even the plants sleep   Just stopped   perfect and unchanged Finally the prince finds the princess lying on her bed   She is truly the most beautiful princess he has ever seen   It has been a very long search   In his reverence and gratitude the prince bends down and kisses the princess gently on the cheek   I lean over and touch my lips very softly to Ally's cheek

My sister leaves for a moment and my lover mouths I love you to me across the rug that once adorned an entrance hall in one of my childhood homes. As I mouth back the same I love you, I catch a glimpse of a painting I once made. Over ten years before, I gave that painting as a wedding present to my sister and her husband. My sister had asked me to be a bridesmaid and I refused. I just couldn't wear the clothes. My painting now hangs next to one of my mother's paintings. I remember how much I once disdained my mother's paintings. They looked like wallpaper, I thought. Now the two paintings on the wall, mine and my mother's, look surprisingly similar. Tonight I feel comforted by the warm colors in my mother's painting. Tonight I forgive my mother. And tonight this apartment holds just the four of us, three women and a child. Do I have all this now? A family with a woman I want to be with and to love through life? I wonder: Are we

really so different, my sister and I? We had the
only house on the block with modern furniture.
Outsiders looking in always thought we had an
impeccable home. And much of what was there
is here, a bit faded, child-worn and spotted,
relics almost.

Ally blinks her eyes and lifts up slowly from the floor
Behold! I call   The princess has woken!   Ally
stretches out one arm then the other   she stands up
I feel new! she exclaims   I feel brand new!   she
takes up her scarf and begins to dance around the
room   The flowers are new! she shouts   I follow
her and the music carries us around the room   Ally
spins and twirls   I'm having a wonderful time! she
exclaims again

"Thanks," my sister says to me with gratitude as
she and my lover walk into the kitchen to wash
the dishes from dinner. In the kitchen, my sister
asks my lover how long we have known each
other. My lover's response disappears under
the music.

I'm getting dizzy Ally tells me   I have to spin until I get
sleepy   she spins until she falls   I'm so sleepy   I
have to go to sleep now   Ally makes the perfect bed
for herself out of the blue scarf   she lies down and
waits for the story to begin again

I KNOW YOU

Just what is that feeling when you walk down a road and you are Elvis and dark eyebrows?   you are your father's and your grandfather's face   you are a young man with extremely sexy buns and you are wanted but hidden somehow   perhaps unattainable   with tight ass and full lips and known by other girl girls on the street   your heart pounds as much as anyone's when you are thrown against a pile of apples and fucked by a long-nosed dark-haired girl and a blonde girl in light fitted clothes   for sure you have on cowboy boots and sunglasses   for sure a perfect white t-shirt under denim   for sure you are much taller than you really are   for sure you drive a truck   and when you walk into a store or an orchard or anywhere   there is a gasp and some woman says "shit" under her breath but the "shit" is perfectly audible as if you are the first woman she has seen in that part of the world because you have walked in on her out of the air and it's not New York City

That's one side of it all

The other side has something to do with the shadow of a mustache on your upper lip   something to do with the run of your years toward 40   the grey streaks through your sideburns   something to do with too much worry and the confidence that overhangs it   something to do with blue and North Greenbush where you happen to be that day when you pass a single apple orchard and stop and get out of your car

OUT

I could go out tonight and pick up a woman who only
wanted to make love to me   I would dress so red
and so soft a rose would not compare to my leg or my
stockinged toes   I could go out tonight and pick up a
straight woman who always wanted to try something
new   like someone I once fell in love with   I could
go out tonight and pick up a man   a thin gay man
about my height who just might hold me until the
morning and rub my back to let me feel his solid hands
because like me he has forgotten what the other sex
really felt like and besides he'd talk about it   I could
go out tonight and pick up a large blonde who would
sit in back of me on a chair   her arms would reach
around me into my crotch   I'd be naked of course
and it might be 90 degrees in Phoenix Arizona and her
hands would be so warm and one of her thighs would
push right up into my anus   I could go out tonight
and pick up my lover who I might pick up any night
right out of our bed   I would let her hold me apart
and put her mouth on me   I would watch with her
one woman harness another on the VCR   I would let
her throw me in the car and ride away with me   one
hand on the wheel   the other between my legs

TV DINNER

A long slow walk and then a kiss   all the more to entice because two gorgeous women in skirts stared breathlessly at each other across a file cabinet in a law office in the middle of corporate America   one woman said she was a lesbian   the other said she was not

What was that? a child asked as she and her mother sat together watching TV in the living room   her mom said she didn't know and turned the TV off   Read a book instead Mom said   she wanted her daughter to have a choice so she took two books down from the shelf: *The Little Engine That Could* and *Horton Hears a Who*

In the darkened TV two women in tight skirts just above the knee had dinner out then left the restaurant to sit thigh to thigh in the car   the driver who was the lesbian said Keep talking   and let her hand creep between her passenger's legs   the passenger tried not to gasp as her clit caught a ringed finger   Later the passenger said and pushed the arm away   but the hale hand answered with a brush against stockinged skin and a voice that said I won't wait

What was that? the child heard in dark sleep where the peach walls and office air over the file cabinet filled with phlox and lupine   what was that?   an engine climbed a mountain up vertical cliffs into a tunnel and she thought   this is me   I am this train surrounded by black air lit with soft fires   and when she woke with her mother's knock on the bedroom door she noticed that the day at first seemed darker than the night

NIGHT CALLS

The first   Hello hello   in deep southern damp
before you have a chance to say wait   she says I
just wanted to tell you that my voice will be a regular
thing   you listen and somehow your lover does not
know or if she does it's OK because every night now
the phone rings at 4 a.m.   I want to tell you that
you are beautiful   Each part of you   No   Don't
say anything   Not a thing   I can see you lying
there   lips close to the woman you love   Don't try to
tell me different because now I'm going to watch you
under the sheets   your breasts cupped gently under
you   Did you know that I'm taking you to St. Louis?
You're going to get on a bus and stay very quiet   I'll
be there next to you   my lips on your head   my
belly bruising you against the seat and my wide hard
legs holding you to my crotch   Don't say anything
Don't ask me who I am   I'm going to lie here now
and touch myself and you just listen and think that you
might be in my arms

You hear her and stay silent in your bed   phone
cupped between ear and chin   her large belly and
large hands round and round   your lover breathes
quietly next to you and the next night the woman calls
again and wraps her hands around you with a slightly
higher voice which kneads strongly into your back
and ass   pushes itself in and stays there until you
fall asleep cradled in her slow swing   you touch
your lover next to you and sleep and wake and sleep
until the moon goes down and the phone rings again
at 4 a.m.

SUITS AND TIES

That was who you were then   Sam   clad in a tie and
one of those cheap boy's suits you found in a store
on 1st avenue at a close-out sale   you tried on one
after the other   5-7 dollars a piece   you bought six
or seven with one thrown in for free   it was as if you
had found the treasury of some glorious bank which
you then took home and tried on for your lover

Now Sam has a tie collection so large it takes up a
whole closet   ten white and three pink cotton shirts
and a few off-white linens and perhaps a celestial blue
the color of your faded jeans   your shirts are lined
up in the closet   all with perfect collars buttoned
just up under your chin   and a collection of splendid
hats   these are your serious clothes to be worn with
thick wool suits   having outgrown the narrow cuts of
boys for the richer drapes of material along the length
of your thigh   cut like the suits of the wealthiest men
you have a closet full of beautiful polished shoes and
linen socks and just the right cotton underwear to fit
your ample butt and thighs and skinny yellow belly

Take off Sam's clothes   one sock at a time   take off
the pants   then there you are   with nothing on your
bottom   the little red or blue jockey underwear pulled
off   your white shirt tails hanging down over your
nakedness   you could be going out for the evening
in suit coat and hat   perhaps you still have on your
tie   and she takes you out through the door into the
night   a lead on your wrist   she has on a slip under
her full clothes and stockings and high heels and it
is the city or the country   you go for a walk like this
and this is what is most important   she takes you to a
tree and ties your hands behind   she kisses you and
rubs her gloved hands up between your thighs   you
watch as she takes off her high heels   you watch as
she slowly pulls off her stockings and dangles them
in front of your face   you watch as she rolls the

94

nylon into itself and picks up your foot and unrolls the stockings up onto your own legs   she pulls them up over your ass and places a high heel on each of your feet   she stares at you and laughs   this is what you really are   this   and she kisses your lips full with her lipstick so now you too have on lipstick   she laughs and calls you a beautiful gorgeous young girl and unties your hands and takes off your jacket and unbuttons your cover of a white shirt   and then there you are standing naked with stockings and high heels and lipstick and you are hers   she reaches into the stockings and fucks you standing up this way   you are to do nothing to her   nothing at all except after when you go back and put on your shirt and your tie and your suit and you will look great and glorious to the girls who pass by   and you will   yes you will find that one woman who walks down the street in a tight-meaning dress and she is the one who will take you out for a walk to the tree where you become her and she becomes god

NORMAL SEX

I'm a housewife every day   or lounger   birdwatcher
a domestic with an apron who places a bowl of fruit
on the table in this perfectly chandeliered hall   one
can't help but notice the dust on everything once it
stops being new   they should deliver the stuff and
come back once a month to wipe it off since I don't
do it and neither do you   not to say that we don't
try   try to eat stir-fry   try to eat grains and tofu and
beans and free-range chicken   it's not to say that
all the best foods taste better followed by a Mounds
bar (dark chocolate only) and salt 'n vinegar potato
chips   and it's not to say that sometimes I hate you
for this life but mostly I love you and it's not your doing
anyway   it's what I was brought up with   white
sinks and clean counters   but I've also seen the
other side   the shit in the hole and your finger in mine

I CAME

On my back on the black-and-white tiled bathroom
floor of a hotel in Madrid   my parents going out
and I had my hand between my legs   they shouted
Goodbye and I shouted Goodbye through the closed
door   never to stop the circular motion of my finger
on my clit

To say goodbye on the sands of Egypt   cradled in
her arms on the improbable back of a camel   her
blonde thighs large around my own   she held the
reins near my crotch and perhaps could feel how hot
I was in the sun as the camel lurched forward over
the sand

I came too   riding in the back of the family car all
dressed in party clothes for a symphony concert
patent leather shoes   heavy wool coat   parents
in the front   seat belt not around my waist but up
through my stockinged legs   as tight as possible
beneath my coat   no one would know how tight as
the car braked to a quick stop and I talked lightly and
practiced as my mother asked me about homework
and a painting at the museum and a piece of news
about an aunt who lived in Paris

I find you talking about Paris when I come to on your
bed   it's not really your mouth I see   or your face
it's still the black-and-white tile   the flash of light
the strong blue seat belt and the pommel of a saddle
on a camel's back

I CAME INTO HER

I came into her and out of her   I came into her and
she died and her eyes fell away   I came into her and
felt my fist widen and turn to stone   felt it fill her and
fall through   I came into her and the force of my arms
held her arched   a bridge   I came into her through
the bulge in my crotch   neither a sock nor a rubber
ball   I laughed with her   I saw a pond of eels   my
belly a boat on hers   I came into her and my lips went
white   I came into her and smelled the flanks of a
horse and piles of manure   the wind slammed into
a forest of pine   I came into her and gorged myself
with mud   tasted earth tasted rocks tasted gems   I
came into her and thirsted for bells and heard hillsides
of pots and pans and birds

GO BACK

Go back now to that boy taken by that girl   there
aren't that many who would want to undress him and
get beneath the suit jacket and the white shirt   to
pass through the short hairs on his scalp   to bust
through the ringworm inside the lesion inside the
rare crook of the little finger   come come now now
through the boy through the fingernail dirt back to the
girl underneath it all and the comecome nownow sunk
and drowned in the great green pond

Home

in

three

days.

Don't wash.

…but sexual pleasure often exacts a high price; sooner or later we pay with years of sorrow for every moment of pleasure. It is not God's vengeance but that of the Devil, the enemy of everything beautiful. Beauty has always been dangerous.

—Reinaldo Arenas, *Before Night Falls*

1.
STARVATION

TRASH

I stopped home at lunch because I left my cock on
the bathroom sink   I found it there upstairs nested
in its harness   condom still on   who did you think
you would fuck that you needed a condom?   a man?
a woman?   I liked that you were ready   a little
ashamed that I was not   I never thought that harness
worked very well but it worked perfectly with you and
maybe I don't need a new one after all   so I rushed
home at lunch afraid that my lover (or is that what I call
you now?) might show up   I looked around for tell-
tale signs in the guest room where we slept   shook
out our two pillows and took one downstairs to the
master bedroom   I know I'll sleep upstairs again
tonight and take that pillow with me to bury my head
where you rested yours   I rolled the condom off the
cock   washed the pink rubber and put the cock and
harness back into their soft cotton bag   I wrapped
the condom in one of our Lipton tea bag covers from
last night   took it with me into the car and stuffed the
package into the now empty bag of vegetable chips
from which you fed me   parsnip   yucca   ruby
taro   that one with a drawing inside   another that
looked and tasted like potato but which you insisted
was not   I finished the chips this morning in the car
taking that condom still full of you out of its Lipton tea
bag cover   unrolling a bit and placing the tip into
my mouth   I tasted latex and lubricant and I tasted
you   and after I was done I rewrapped the condom
stuffed the bundle back into the empty chips bag and
put it all into an old brown paper lunch sack   I had
to go to the bank so I threw the whole thing out in the
lobby under where one writes deposit slips

STARVATION

I thought about the morning and waking up for you to see me older and lined perhaps that is why I left your hotel room so early   3:42 a.m.   I was tired and cold and wanted to get under the covers of your bed but did not want to wake you   perhaps that was too intimate a gesture for what we had done and what we had done was not the intimacy of early mornings or the light of aging faces or a quiet sleep in each other's arms   we accomplished something else of course and I did kiss you on the head and smelled my fingers full of you   and maybe it was better that I left and walked through the yellow-lighted halls of your floor a renovation in progress   walls half-painted and torn with room numbers taped crookedly onto doors ceiling lights and wires hanging down   claw-like and scraped   your nightmare you said   details you see I remember   I remember how I walked into the elevator wondering if my clothes were all on and zippered and buttoned in case I met someone   I did not meet anyone even on my already renovated floor   was I now renovated too as I entered my room quietly without lights so as not to wake my sleeping roommate?   as I lay tossing on my bed with the smell of you?   with the fact that I did not come and wanted you again and how starved I must be   when I saw you the next day you completely distracted me from what I had to do   and now it is two weeks and your package came today and I held it with the rest of the mail against my chest and pushed it up the stairs of the deck with me behind as I might hold your back to my chest and push you forward up and into my house through the living room and onto the bed   I am starved   I found myself turning off the radio in the car and felt your head in my lap   I am starved   last night I kissed your ear before I went to sleep   I am starved I do not want to eat   starved   when I try to pray my fingers are your fingers on the back of my neck

ADRIENNE

I'm sure I had your note held close in the breast pocket of my jacket when I left for the evening but it must have slipped to the floor of the auditorium as I took out my wallet to write down someone's number when I realized the note was gone I could only think of who might pick it up   was it the very butch security guard I saw at the reception who later came to lock up for the evening?   was it the baby dyke at the college working off her scholarship sweeping up behind the seats?   or was it the pepper-haired academic who sat mutely next to me with lined face   pumpkin blazer charcoal wool pants   purple scarf not unlike the one Adrienne wore around her neck?   one of them for sure would look down and notice the plain party-sized envelope   would pick it up and lift out that small folded square of paper

Last night I lay in bed and tried to reconstruct your words   I barely remember the 'pounce' as you called it   but I do remember you on top of me   gently at first   and how your face looked as you rubbed yourself in cotton knit pants slowly against the fly of my jeans   and yes you did kiss me and forced my own kisses out of my mouth   I got lost at your nipple your skin strangely rough   and would have gone on and on   drawing blood   had you not stopped me

Your note   only a few phrases really   but perhaps enough for one unknown woman who might reach down to pick up a stray piece of paper   who might read it again this morning and know of hunger from the floor of an auditorium where Adrienne's words still charge the air

DRIVE

I want to drive forever and to keep talking to you but
really I think I am talking to me and some higher angel
who suddenly wears a suit and a tie and who whispers
in my ear: This is the life you deserve   she follows
me everywhere these days and by the time I went to
sleep last night my dog had gotten her head on your
pillow and it smelled more of her than of you   I tried
to catch a glimpse of you anyway and saw your ass
where we walked up the road   I watched my hand
as it cupped your left cheek   your upper thigh as it
folded over my fingers   now the sun is at my back
lowering skies ahead   golds   dark darks and
reds and brilliant light   you used to play the piano
and when I asked about your favorite piece you were
caught off guard and could not remember   Bartók
you said   an unexpected answer   but maybe not

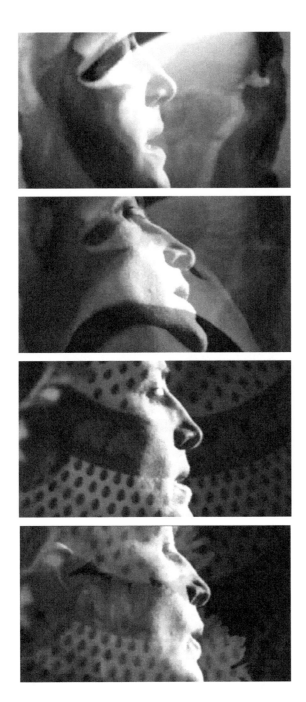

MAP

I walk into your light-filled house and a map slowly
forms in my mind   you are here in this large plain
chair talking to me   oh you are here   sitting at
this table with the one beautiful green leg   eating
dinner with the illuminated globe of your TV   oh
you are here sitting in the couch remembering how
we lay belly to belly listening to music   oh here
explorer walking by your lover at her desk and here
through the narrow hall to the right where two people
cannot pass without pushing each other up against
the wall   oh here you are at the linen closet replacing
the red towel now washed of our blood   now here
in the laundry room washing your black underwear or
brushing your teeth before bed or touching your sore
insides   oh here you are in the kitchen with the faint
smell of gas and the border of iridescent green tiles
here   opening the refrigerator with its perfectly
squared survey of magnets and charts   here you
are warming and drinking your Chinese herbs your
soymilk in tea and here you are touching the petals of
your rose   here   the dining room   uninhabited   a
passage between bedroom and bathroom to wash to
carry used tampons to pee to brush our teeth   here
you are on your tall bed   your dog buried in the
covers of your matted cotton quilt   here looking for
your clothes   here setting your clock   here turned
on your side toward the wall   here I hold you from the
back   watch your smooth pink cheek   here I enter
you   your one leg raised   my map

PRAYER

(I started to write & the letter upset me & I called and
cried & you washed the sheets & had me pray.)

So you said   and yes I like lipstick   not on me   on
you   you cried on the phone   overwhelmed by my
love and yours   by the all too many words   by your
days which go by now too fast with too much work and
not enough time   by your cold   by and for desire
you cried in your home sitting in your wide blue chair
next to the low table low chair and the couch we made
love on which now holds your lover passed out on thick
wine   you cried and asked if I was sleeping upstairs
tonight in the guest room where we slept before you
drove off into the dark   you cried because I said no
because I said I washed the sheets and tried to tell you
why   because I woke thinking it was time to sleep
in a cooler place   to sleep in the bed downstairs
where I had slept for many years with my lover   on
the side of the bed I chose near the window for quick
escape   my back turned from the wide expanse of
the mattress   to wake and to look out at my pine
tree and the empty bird feeder and everything that was
safe and everything that kept me separate and alone

The night you called and cried I did sleep downstairs
but before I slept I also prayed   and I prayed again
when I got up   and in the new morning you said (on
the phone again)   Look but don't touch   and for the
first time claimed me for your own

MEETING

Last night I ate like normal   papers all over the place
TV on mute   dirty dishes spread around   and this
afternoon I sit in a meeting and there are hundreds
of speeches and charts to say what could be said in
one sentence   I am not the only one writing during
this presentation   there is one other and I do not
believe she is taking notes   but I wonder   does she
describe the sudden jerks of desire as kisses come
close to the folds of her lover's ass and cunt?   I
sit at a table beneath the podium   the people in
the audience can clearly see me as I write   I feel
as if I am kissing you in public   and now the other
woman has stopped writing and has folded her letter
(I can see that it is a letter now) while someone at the
podium talks about change   this is what is being
said: #1) Be honest with yourself   #2) Participate
#3) Be compassionate   #4) Only with change can
we survive into our future   now there is a video
playing and still the smell of you

RULES

Rule One: Raise Your Hand   Daniel is writing not listening and I tell him to listen because this review is mostly for his benefit but if I were him I probably would go on writing   Rule Two: Listen To Others   Janey calls out across the room and I tell her to raise her hand and she does and when I call on her she has nothing to say   Rule Three: Talk Nicely To Others   I explain the difference between joking and teasing and when teasing turns mean and starts to make another person mad   and when the other person gets mad like Derrick was at Daniel when Daniel teased him Derrick might want to punch Daniel in the arm Derrick did punch Daniel in the arm   which brings us to Rule Four: Keep Your Hands To Yourself   which is when the phone rings and somehow I think it might be you so I keep talking about teasing   a little louder now so perhaps you can hear me   how teasing can be a good thing and how far it might go before falling over the edge into cruelty   I have someone else take over the review and I find your voice on the phone   I put my finger into my free ear in order to hear you better through the classroom noise and the beating of my heart   I don't understand at first   Just say Yes or OK   you have to repeat your words three times Just say Yes or OK   then I hear you whisper   Will you get hard for me?   I say I will   and you say   Just say Yes or OK   I finally get it and say   Yes   you say   Will you force your cock down my throat?   Yes Will you see me again?   Yes   and then you say goodbye and I hang up the phone and wonder if my face has turned white or red   the speech teacher who is leading the class says Rule Five: Stay In Your Seat   in my mind I see you start to get up   Stay In Your Seat I say to you under my breath as I stand up and smooth down my pants   Stay In Your Seat   I see you follow and I repeat   Stay   as I take your mouth into my hands

PAINTER

You are to remember my lessons well   my lips next to
your ear   my hands on your shoulders   I say: Look
it is not *like* anything   not an ocean or a snowstorm
not a metal door   *it is* that black dot and the sharp
left corner and the nail and the two fasteners bottom
and left then the space in between   it is the shimmer
of the surface where one's eyes cannot rest   it is the
smudge that you found near the bottom right   the
shadow underneath   my hand as it bruises your arm
my voice as it says *it is   it is*   my lips now crushing
your cheek in this room of snowstorms because these
paintings are not as good as the others and *are* like
Antarctica

TELEPHONE

I asked you to see if you were wet and yes you were
and I told you to keep your finger there and you said
No   No   Keep your finger there I said again   no
so quietly you said no   and then you said you had
to get off the phone and you hung up and I was
left breathless   thinking I had finally gone too far
stepped over some line of demarcation between us to
the place you would stop opening before me   I held
my head in my hands   pleaded   felt lonelier than
ever before   as if you were just some fantasy of mine
and then the phone rang again and it was you "to say
a proper goodbye"   no apology but an explanation
your girlfriend had simply walked into the room   this
time to my enormous joy

SNAKE

I straddle the car of your train and the platform   one
foot on each   and hold open the door as it tries to
close on my back   I will keep you   not let you go   I
will show off my strength and I am ten   my sister and
I visit a friend on her farm and we play games around
the pond   I decide to show this girl with long dark
braids exactly what I can do   so when I see a large
snake swimming across the water I run to the other
side and wait for it to climb out   my sister yells for
me to stop and the snake is already half-way down its
hole when I grab its tail   I have to use both hands
and rock back on my heels to pull it out which I do but
the snake snaps its head around and sinks its teeth
into the ring finger of my right hand refusing to let go
even when I try to shake it off   finally it does let go
and my sister cries and says How could you and the
girl with the braids stares at me silent   I am bleeding
but proud as they march me back to the house   the
girl's mother calls my mother then a doctor to make
sure the snake isn't poisonous (three puncture marks
or two)   and I turn to grin at that girl as I now grin at
you and push with all my might to hold back that door
and the leaving of your train

SHOPPING

I wonder now if the cock I bought for you is too big
I will become a collector and there will be a library
for you to pick out the one that suits you best on any
particular day   big   small   inbetween   generic
penis-like   thick   thin   various colors of flesh
and sizes for your ass   I walked past the posters
at Lincoln Center and felt a shock in my cunt like you
rolled over inside me and the feeling stayed sharp and
only intensified at the store where I tried on harnesses
in the dressing room with sample dildoes and only a
candle for light   I could see the outline of the cock
and I could feel it inside you and at a certain point
I did take off my pants and tried on everything over
my underwear because I wanted to make sure the fit
was right so I would be able to fuck you hard and
long   I carried my shopping bag next to me and on
the subway   three girls stood above me so involved
in their conversation they noticed nothing about me
or my bag   *I can't believe you go out with that boy*
He's a Nazi   He likes Hitler   He loves Hitler   No
He's not a Nazi   But he does love Hitler   Alfred
was a Nazi and he was sick   three college girls
riding up the West Side   I pulled my shopping bag
closer to my seat and one of the girls talked about
her roommate   *She's from the farm and she knows*
nothing   so one day she was looking for something
to do and I asked her to make my bed   She said I
don't know how to make a bed   So I asked her to
iron my shirts   She said I don't know how to iron
shirts   She knows nothing   Maybe where she's
from they use stones for toilet paper   That's what
happens on the farm   they probably don't have
beds to make   I tried not to stare   what did they
know?   I thought about my new harness and cock
and my eye caught the gaze of a woman in a business
suit   I shifted my bag and the woman sighed at
me and cracked her gum as if she was someone who
knew

HOW DOES IT SOUND?

How does it sound when you come?   I hear you on the telephone at 3:00 p.m. on a Saturday   I tell you that I hold you open with the white of your ass spread in my face   the mud of a field fissured in an earthquake strained then collapsed   how does it sound when you come?   I am so far inside you I no longer care if I tear you apart   I am only a part of a hundred trains   like the rush of buffalo stomped up your groin at the edge of a cliff   I will fuck you hard and then harder again and I will never stop   I will turn you around just before you fall to spread you further   right up into your liver your spleen your chest your heart your lungs until you cannot breathe   I hold onto your shoulders   my hands around your neck   you are falling darling   completely beside yourself   you are at that edge and all you need is just one push   fires on the rocks below and you wail as you fall hearing the screech of owls   you scratch my face apart   strain at your ties and pull your legs up and tight and you claw the sheets   you clench and begin to moan tighter around me send five shudders you no longer have a choice your moans turn higher your nails pulled out lips nipples clamped you scream now you fight you thrash you shatter you find boy find girl you call you weep my name

THE NEED TO FUCK

The need to fuck comes over me as I walk through
department stores and touch the sheer clothing I
would buy for you if you ask   as I feel the damp
of your mound through the cotton panties hanging in
layers on the racks   as I stare at stockings with lace
at the thighs where I would graze along until I find
the soft dwelling between thigh and cunt   my berth
the shift from silk to the touch of skin where I would
pray for hours   the need to fuck comes over me as
I talk to you on the telephone and hear the need in
your voice   when I tell you to push your pants down
around your thighs and tell you to spread your legs
the need to fuck comes over me as I tell you to touch
yourself   as I tease your breasts with my cock   just
out of your reach   the need to fuck   as I watch the
crack between the cheeks of your ass   the need to
fuck how wet you are   the need to fuck as you start
to come and I go far up inside you and you cannot
stop the need to fuck here in the dress department
here behind the racks

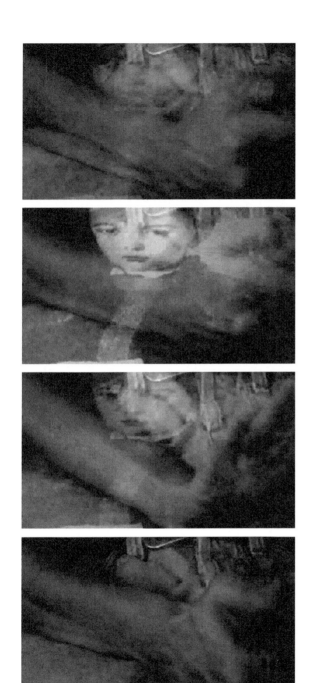

MEN'S

I wait at a train crossing for the train to go by and I
have on men's underwear today   because after all I
am a small wiry man   I am also a woman who likes
how this underwear hugs my ass and legs and how
it's bigger in the crotch to hold my cock   I bought
them on Sunday in the men's underwear department
at Macy's where I saw again how much better made
even common men's wear is than women's   after
previously spending time in the women's lingerie
department picking out a gift for you   so I have
pouchless and pouched to test you with and I love
box cars   dry lumber   gas cans   crude oil
here's one empty   with your initial carved inside a
thousand times   I'm not kidding   I also love the
backs of trucks   I stare at rear doors on the highway
smudged with their owner's hands

HOME IN THREE DAYS.
DON'T WASH.

Napoleon to Josephine

I am driving to you and I will drive all the way to New
York   through the long round of the earth   the
plains   the wheat   through the hills of Ohio and the
darkening cities of Pittsburgh and Philadelphia and
Trenton   don't wash   I am listening to music   loud
I can't stop   I am driving right into you with my foot
my heart my fist   the faster I go the closer I am to
you   I only slow down for police cars hidden behind
the corners of the highway   behind well-placed trees
and planned hillocks   I won the last battle   I won in
all my short and skinny frame   at least 1500 hearts
because of you they saw me   because of you they
saw what I have to offer   they cried in ecstasy when
I tore off their clothes   they cried when I sliced open
their throats   they cried when they saw everything I
can give you   they wanted my hardness   the curl
of my lip   they wanted the murderer in me   don't
wash   I want a weeks worth of you wet   I want
the same underwear   the same sour smell   layers
of it thick   the soak and musk of you   I too am
acquiring mud and the scum of desire   my cock has
not come down yet from thinking about you   through
entire days of battle   don't wash   it's becoming
night now   I see pinks and blue   a deer by the
side of the road   I'm driving south now into the
constant drench of you   the earth on my left shoulder
don't wash   don't wash the books out of your hands
don't wash the telephone you've held between your
chin and my mouth   don't wash away the meal you
had this morning   the orange juice on your chin
don't wash the history of the breaths you have taken
in my absence out of your mouth   I want to know
them   all the churches and all the stores smell me
as I go by   they smell my desire and the force of my

lips   they smell how I hold my breath   the inside of
your shoes   that white layer now at the fold where
your thigh touches your labia   that punk   your hair
matted   waiting   wait that long   that much   I
want you not to move and therefore not to live except
to feel the force of my hand on your forehead   around
your jaw   taste my mouth   yellow lines   white
lines   a horse in the road   I am not tired   I will drive
through the night   I will not eat   the dirt still caked
around my fingernails   this is what they want   all
of them   they smell what happens with you   that I
a woman   have something to offer a woman   that I
have something to take her with   do not wash   you
will crawl over me with the mud of your days   with
all the slime and smell and wild leaves of them   and
I will fill myself on the sourness of your ass and your
cunt as they ride between my thumb and forefinger
I will lick you clean   all of that will be mine   I have
fasted for days waiting

In the end I will wash you and you will rise out of the
bath   sweet smelling   to sleep and wake again
perhaps you will wake to tell me how much I stink
because I have not washed even longer than you
you will say: you think you can come in here looking
like that?   you think you can come in here with the
blood of all those women on your hands?   you think
you can tear apart the world then come to tear me
apart?   you think you can seduce everyone with your
words then come and ravish me?   no   not now
not with your stinking lousy little man self   how small
you are   how thin   how unbelievably proud   those
arms couldn't fuck a pigeon could they?   those lights
that stop sign   this fork in the road   you would have
me?   how could you walk into our house this way?

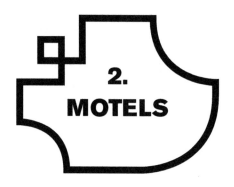

2.
MOTELS

DAYS INN

It was astonishing to walk into room 233 at the Days
Inn   the door open for us   to turn on the lights
and to close the curtains   to see you first locked
into that tan recliner as I sat on the (slightly darker)
tan carpet   my back up against the coarse blue
bedspread   to smell disinfectant and to drink bitter
tea   to feel the minutes of our short afternoon slip
away into nervousness and the prints on the off-white
walls   then how you lay down on the bed and I
lay next to you   to kiss   no   to talk   to get
comfortable with each other again   we heard raised
voices from somewhere   from the side or overhead
we couldn't figure out where   perhaps a meeting or
ten TVs   screaming children or a gathering of boys to
watch the football game   these were all possibilities
as gradually the voices got so loud I called the front
desk to complain   the desk clerk said the voices
were coming from below   something religious for
sure   evangelists or a revival meeting   I told the
clerk that I would call her back if we needed to move
then you asked me to turn off the hard lights and I
did and lay back down next to you and then on top
of you and I finally forgave myself for letting you wait
at the train station   I remember you turned me over
and how delirious I became at your touch and at a
certain point I was overwhelmed with the desire to
enter you and all the while beneath us they called
on the Lord   they called for salvation   the desk
called and out of breath I answered and said we were
fine and did not want to move and it was true   the
room had become as if lighted by candles and we
lay on a sacred bier accompanied by hosannas and
hallelujahs   and the chalice of your scent   the icon
of your face   the idols of your breasts in black lace
the staff of your finger in my ass and my cock in your
cunt   our coming joined from below by shouts and
applause and the exalted blessings of the possessed

CHELSEA THIRTEEN

I like our little white room in this soiled hotel and want
an entire life to fit into our short five hours   the desk
clerk irritates you by talking on the phone too long and
when you ask I say choose the back not the street
our room dirty but with the light of Italy and I think I
should take you right off but we talk and you ask do
you like teenagers and I say no I like women and you
look away as if your feelings are hurt   and in the
time it takes to get you back I see the blonde of who
you want me to see this afternoon   the pubescent
13-year-old   I see your thighs still long and boy-like
your small breasts   the pink in your cheek and your
lips shell-like red   the inside of a conch   there in
Maine   there upstate   the shell now on your mantle
I want her as I want you   my little girl   want to put
you on my lap   want you to sit on my cock   quiet
now   want to rock you   hold you   take you home
lay you down on the leaves   watch you fight yourself
shot through and taken no matter what you say

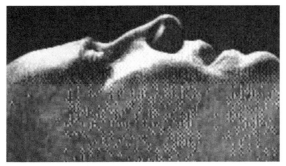

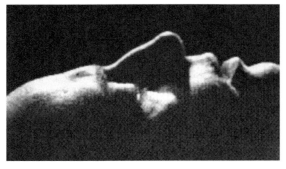

129

FRIENDSHIP INN

Early this time at the train station   I finish my tea and
your train comes in right on schedule but on track 3
instead of track 1   and you appear   traveling light
as usual   and cold   your face relaxed with a bit of
a devilish grin   we drive what seems miles hoping
for an open room and you persuade me that you will
appear more convincing (more femme?) to the desk
clerk on a busy New Year's morning   I wait   unable
to see you through the reflections in the glass door
except for your legs in your jeans beneath your jacket
and already I want you   I have wanted you since you
got off the train   since talking to you on the phone
last night   I have wanted you for days   and you have
been successful even though the place filled up late
last night with revelers not wanting to drive   we have
been given the keys to room 126 but I take you to
find tea first then to our room which we have trouble
finding because it follows 127 and 128 completely
out of sequence which is how you fell into my life   I
like this room in the back of the motel   here with no
reason   a bit dreary on such a beautiful day   but
we turn day into night and you are childlike   sleepy
playing with me   we wrestle   I am thrilled to feel
your body again   to laugh with you   here you are
curled into me   letting me glimpse your new panties
and bra   uncomfortable you say but bought for me
here you are talking to me   turning on the TV   little
girl today   here is your breast in my teeth   here
you are making me guess what you want   flattened
against me   and I find my finger in your ass   and
here you are loving me   touching me through my
underwear   I don't want you to go too fast and you
comply but anything would be too fast   and here you
are again struggling against me as I ask you to take
more and I do not stop until you say enough and you
take more than you ever have

WATERGATE

You called it our first house   the little octagonal
building on a hill over the bridge   brick with a red
door and white trim   I thought I liked it better than
the others until you told me how much it cost   we
paid for a whole night but stayed only an afternoon
right away I pulled up your shirt and placed my cock
against your neck like a knife   I stripped off your
pants with the orange juice stains and saw your lace
panties and bra and how exposed and wanting you
looked   I kissed you and held your nose so you really
could not breathe this time   I turned you over and
entered you from behind then let you suffer for not
touching you   you know what happened don't you?
when I sat down in the shower before going out that
night   I looked down and there were your lips on the
inside of my thigh   your mark

HENRY VAN

There was a mudslide at Dobb's Ferry so you must come up the Harlem line instead of the Hudson   you call before you leave to say you are ill   do you really want to come?   I thought I heard a hint of something in your voice   we dodge obstacles like the quarterback now in the end zone who dances and lifts his head to heaven   but I do find you later at the train station and we drive and discover a sweet motel in an unlikely place   a dark room for which we pay money to be with each other on a sunny day   you worry and we do not touch right away   you get up and pace and turn on the TV and divert yourself from me as I do from you with talk   for hours we talk and I tell you that I do not want to get so used to leaving you after loving you that I do not stop wanting you   I do not stop the night before nor the night after and the night after that   so I say and so it happens that it is the right thing to stop your talk with my finger in your mouth   the right thing to stop the pacing the diversion the TV   the right thing to give you more than you think you can take the right thing at the back of your throat at your nipple and finally at your clit   the right thing to drink orange juice in between   to fuck you again   and finally to let you take me and to hear you whisper to your little boy who you ask to sit on your lap   it's the way you push him down by his left shoulder as he tries to reach up and touch you   the way you lift your large full breasts just out of the reach of his mouth and hands   the way you make him struggle and do not give and finally he does reach you and after I think yes   let us return to this place   to the whole of you and me   meeting for 20 dollars apiece at the Henry Van along a highway near the train somewhere upstate

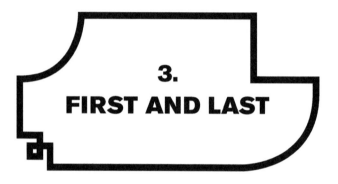

3.
FIRST AND LAST

TELEPHONE II

(I was out to dinner and wanted to get up and say to all of them: I am in love with someone who is not sitting at this table.)

You tell me this over the phone and in the next breath ask me to be a young man off the street when it's hot and I am sweaty and I have followed you home   I will do anything for you and tell you that I watch you secretly as you bathe then lotion yourself   put on silk panties and camisole   I will do anything for you and suddenly I grab your arm and drag you into the bedroom   I tell you that you will never do what you have done   that you will never again walk in front of me and tantalize me   I will force open your legs   I will touch your clit and tell you that you are shameful and that you will not be separate from me   that I will take you any moment I want   do you understand?   you ask me over the phone to be a young man off the street and after you come you order me to lie down   I will do anything for you but this is more difficult   OK I say   besides I have to pee and you   a woman   will not let me for hour after hour until it becomes unbearably painful and your voice takes over and you hold my cunt in your hand and you will punish me severely if I can't hold it any longer   you say you will parade me around the bedroom in a dress   that only you will have this and know as I walk around the world in suits and ties and white shirts   you will tell me exactly what I am   a woman and a girl and that I am also some young boy who you have taken off his bicycle into the woods and shown him your cock and played with his little dick that you show him how to get hard and show him how you get hard and at some time he gets frightened and you turn him over and fuck him in the ass and bring him off with your hand yanking on his dick and now you are some tough ravishing woman who loves me   grime and all   who will tear it all apart for me   one strand at a time   who will put it all back

BE CAREFUL

You were a wench when we talked this morning and I am on my way to work   my cunt is so hot and I am afraid because of what you said on the phone   Be careful you said   You know what I am   I wanted to say buy Doc Marten's but buy high heels too   you said Be careful   I am an aging drunk   my blood seized and I thought how could I be so stupid and how do I stop this   Well me too I said   if you want to compare apples and apples   and besides some part of me thinks I'm safe

FRIDAY NIGHT

I came to you Friday night through your door through
the early evening through blocks I traveled up and
down four times and watched your windows dark and
waited for you and I came to you finally   carrying
heavy bags   and there you were   smile and pain
through the smile and you turned away not wanting
me to see but I did see your wool coat your sleepy
eyes your white head your lips shuddering through
me and I held you and said There you are   and the
smell of scotch was clear and I shouldered away the
anger that you were ready to pass out   I wanted you
anyway and asked if you wanted to eat   you said I'm
drinking dinner   Bring me some scotch   Where
is the scotch? you asked me until I said Stop asking
and took you into the living room where we sat down
the room looked smaller the couch squat and call me
darling   we kissed and the smell of booze repulsed
and drew me at the same time   I wanted all of you
pores   head   tears crying into my shirt   I took you
and loved you   and you fell asleep   we both did
after making sure everything was alright

HOME

For S.H.W.

I'm coming home now through the woods and thinking
what I might give you today on your birthday   the girl
who put a card on a red door in a college dormitory
and began to teach me about love whether she knew
what she was doing or not   it began with a hand with
a voice with a hello and I began for the first time to
fall to wait for your light step to come down the stairs
now a full doubling of time and I am ever grateful that
you taught me what you did   which was to take me
by the hand   to touch my ear with your lips   to
turn away   to flirt with the boys   to have me shake
for you at the breakfast table with jealousy and desire
at the piano   on soft rugs sitting by the fire drinking
B&B   it began with the way you brushed your hair
and rosemary and the smell of you after a shower   it
began with letter upon letter that I ran to the mailbox
for at my family's house   it began with giving you all
the power   it began in concerts in woolen coats in
long walks through the snow   you taught me at 18
what it meant to love   you taught me desolation and
how finally even desolations   the farmhouse where
you left me   pass away

ART DECO

A piano in a room and a cabinet   closed   music
books   someone's Bach partitas   folk songs and
children's easy pieces   I am visitor here   the room
too hot   a desiccated chamber with an art deco
theme   fat matching blue and red armchairs and a
meticulously shined silver ashtray which I use to block
the door from the cats   my eyes water now from
the dust because I have taken the mattress out of the
couch and placed it on the floor   there are books to
read   movies to watch   I try to find recourse in the
hot dry air   mostly I wait   sometimes so stranded
by desire I can do nothing but attend to objects
candles   ashtray   couch   piano   a bed on the
floor and I see your thigh   one leg bent   one knee
up   there my cock hidden in its bag   here my hand
waiting to sink into and become a deeper part of you

MORNING LOVE

Morning love   but I could have gone on all day where
I had you pinned and held in all places   I had you
yet the day had to be gone to work   to be caught in
the possibilities of discovery by your girlfriend or mine
the day had to take my bag and hide it in your office
and the day had me walk the streets of New York buy
books drink coffee write in public places   I saw a
friend for lunch and my nose bled badly   I walked
into a stationery store where the clerk (miraculously)
let me use the bathroom   I got into my car and drove
out to Long Island to a party for my first ever love 20
years past and found some regret some carrots some
dip and diet coke some nostalgia her husband and
some truth   the day had me come back at midnight
to find you exhausted   you wore new lingerie for me
which I could barely enjoy because you would not let
me see your breasts   I did see your ass in a black
lace thong and I loved you through that then decided
I did not want you to have it so easy   even if it took
3 weeks I wanted you to remember how I turned you
over and looked at your ass but you were somehow
far away and it did not seem to matter and because
my neck was breaking I turned you over again and
sucked you off and felt like I was in the sea off the
coast of Labrador   the next morning you found me
and I saw my chest thin and barely boy-formed and
you thought I might be too skinny and you took me as
a boy and I came hard on my back   but there was
scarcely time to let you explore me when I had to go
back into the living room to get my cock like a person
running full force over a cliff-trap finding himself in
mid-air still running still shooting light and semen but
now not into your open mouth   I retrieved my cock
and strapped it on   pulled my sweatpants over and I
could see my hard-on as I ran back with the lube and
got to the bedroom to find the new tube was sealed
and needed a pin or a sharp instrument to open the
plug and that did it   I got angry with the time going

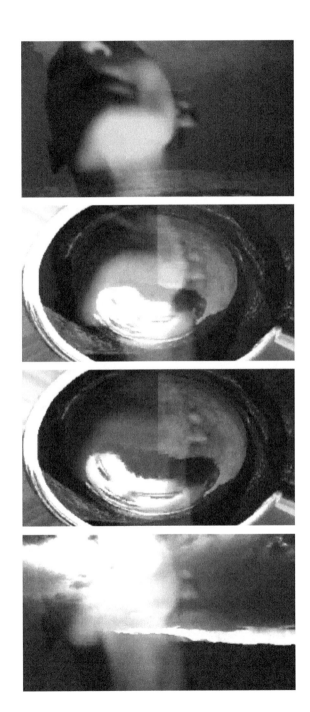

by and we had already canceled breakfast and I threw up my hands and could do nothing but stomp back to the living room dick flapping to find the other already-opened lube which I did find and came back and in my anger made you suck my cock and told you not to get me frustrated   I fucked your throat and wanted to choke you into having me into being mine into revealing everything inside out   then I fucked you hard in your cunt and my cock could have been fatter and shorter like you prefer and for a moment you did forget everything   I sweated and worked and rode you and my cock came out twice and each time it was a little more difficult to get back in then I turned you over and took you in the ass while I touched your clit and you came and then we were done and suddenly it was very late and the dogs had not even been out and we were both afraid of your lover coming home and we had to leave so I ran into the bathroom and showered a short time much shorter than I would have liked and rushed out and took the dogs and one would not poop but that was too bad and I tried to call some friends but no one was home and it was all too much and I had heavy bags and make sure everything is out and there you go and we walk to the car   did we miss anything?   a pair of dirty underwear?   my toothbrush?   you looked at me in the car and said I don't know what's going to happen already I heard the distance in your voice   I'm late for work you said and I dropped you off to pick up orange juice and we all stop drinking and feeling bad about ourselves eventually is what I thought and what I thought is that a letter would be coming from you that would say stop   don't talk   don't make love to me on the phone   that's enough   forget I ever said I loved you   forget all of it   I cried when you got out and shut the door   I tried not to show my face but you knew and goodbye   it's too much and goodbye and I stopped to get coffee which was very bitter and left to drive upstate and that was it   I cried again when I finally walked into my house at the snow and the sweetness of my dogs and the great emptiness

142

and the tightness in my chest   and that was two
days ago   and that was the sound of two-and-a-
half months pinging between my head and heart like a
pinball or a tiny missile of lead which finally shot out of
my lungs as I panicked and screamed into the cold air
for my German Shepherd who I thought might be lost
and goodnight   my dog did come back and now for
two more nights I say goodnight   and thankyou you
said   and thankyou

GIFT

I found your gift in my bag this morning   a shudder
and a thank you and I think of what you can give to me
and of what you can hold back   and now some old
blue man turns around inside me and gathers like my
fist into you   he curls in on himself and sucks his own
cock   he plays his cards right and censors his words
I lay in bed last night with a fever and tried to breathe
the walls were moving and I closed my eyes and what
I heard was the rain and what I heard was the back
of your neck and the rub of you next to me   the
stand straight and back   the older lined business-like
face that is you and your heart today   what I heard
was the sound of ropes down the mountain calling for
rescue   what I heard was the phlegm in my throat
because suddenly I cannot talk   suddenly I cannot
have full freedom to stream out to you   to be caught
and heard and wrestled with   suddenly

144

WHEN BAD IS GOOD

When bad is good when we are in room 626 of the Chelsea Hotel and I am a 35-year-old husband and father and you are a thirteen-year-old babysitter when I make you suck my dick when I am some boy disgusted at how wet you are and I make you ashamed for wanting so much   when bad is good when I put my cock to your throat when you are a man and I am a little boy and you suck me off when you are a woman my mother humiliating me with dresses and stockings when bad is good   when I neglect everything else in my life to hear your call in the night when I wait endlessly for your voice and the moment I will see you when I pack this huge cock for you while I write only turned on by the way it digs into my clit   when bad is good when pain from a leather spanking when aching for you when you are absent when subversion when the high song when losing my home for the sake of freedom   when bad is good when a lie gives you human time to figure out what you want or what to do when trees lose their leaves for the winter and there is no more food in the garden

STOP

(Here is what else I know. You are going to stop this someday.)

Stop what I ask and how?   perhaps it's not what or
how you think   you are going to stop this someday
stop listening   stop talking   stop desire   stop my
heart   stop the drench of you   stop the sound of
your voice   stop the tug of your hands on my ears
stop the fullness of your cover   stop what?   you are
going to stop this someday   stop the plains   stop
the herd   the thunder   stop the way you smell   stop
your wet   your cry   your anger   you are going to
stop this someday   the shots   the impetuousness
stop what?   the lies   the hiding   the secrets   you
are going to stop this someday   the darkness   the
wrestling with strong booze   will I slap you?   shake
you?   throw you up against the car?   will I barge
into your house   pull the hair out of your head and tell
everything to your lover?   will I reach for you in your
dreams and say come?   and will you follow and live
with me on a different mountain?   someday you will
stop this stop listening stop following stop reaching
stop acknowledging just how bad   just how human

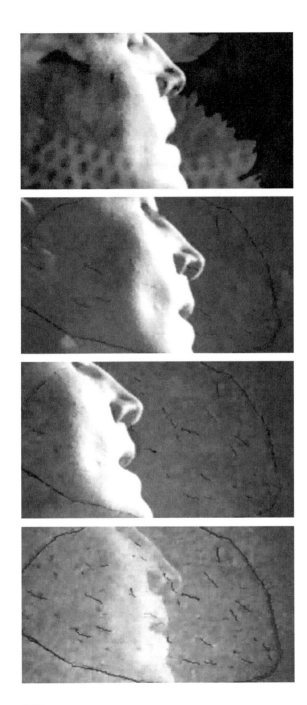

147

EXCEPT I DO

Except the ramble   your voice in my ear   the razor
the black hair the submission the gratification   your
hand without question   except the roll of you   the
harsh whisper of your admonition   except my fist
inside you my cup my packed hunger my wait   I
don't think you know the rot the heave the gaze the
attention the confidence the lesson learned well   but
I do   but I crave but I lie back but I take but I jump
out in front but I seethe

FOUNTAIN

The snow falls relentlessly this afternoon and I will leave here to find you   I will walk through the ice walk through the whole world and bang through the insistent dryness and the insistent wish to see myself dead   I will find my power again with you   two notes of the chickadees to guide me through the snows like they did in Vermont 15 years ago when I learned to occupy my time by walking one step then the next then the next and three tiny birds calling my name just above my head   what finds you this hour? do you hear the soft swish of my skis as they travel through the new snow?   what steers you?   the numbers on your computer?   your taxes and the work you brought home   torn pieces of figures and paper?   I carry your gift of a one-armed turtle as the one solid piece of intimacy that holds me to life   it rests hard rubber in my pocket   uncomfortable when I drive but keeping me awake on slippery roads where the driveway leads out of here to the fountain just on the other side

HER DEVASTATED FACE

Was it the blonde curls surrounding her face?   the
burn?   the touch on the shoulder?   the grateful
smile at my invitation?   was it what I wrote in the
book?   her lips untouched and clear?   was it
not having to hide my own blemishes?   the
awkwardness as I spread my legs on the back of a
chair and knocked down a soda bottle?   was it
her experience with boys?   her fondness for her
mother?   the description of her fight with her boss?
that she was so able?   was it her basketball team?
was it the prospect of a woman's touch?   the low-
cut dress?   the lace underneath?   was it the kind
laugh?   was it the red twist of her lipstick?   was
it the state of want and absence I live with day after
day?   or was it her devastated face   each pore
pretending to be clean and wary and seductive at the
same time   her devastated face   where I would
place my bottom lip with a trace of gratitude that
might just grow   her devastated face   immobile
the desire to be clear   and her somewhat stupefied
former boyfriend   waiting   he looked lessened
like a warning   his suit too big

151

QUIET LIFE

I came to the door of your quiet life and said in a quiet voice hello I am your lover's lover when your lover answered the door   Hello   She has been trying to keep you from me and me from you   hello in case you wanted to know about me here I am but you probably don't because if you did you would have already seen since it is right here in front of your face and I know how she can smile and I know how it can all be a façade and I know it scared me did it ever scare you?   I just wanted to shake your hand   I wanted to feel the hand of you   to feel why she never writes   I wanted to know the catch where she cannot get a smooth sentence out of her heart   to know the sound of her fate or at least how long her hair is and if she keeps it tied back with a barrette or a rubberband do you like barrettes?   I have seen the inside of your house   I have been under the covers of your bed   I have admired two paintings out of 20 in your home I have drunk out of your glass and your saucers   I have eaten the cottage cheese you had for lunch   I have sat heavily on your couch   I have done much much more and I wanted even more than that and I am not proud of any of it   let me shake your hand   let me caress your brow   let me let you stare at me   let me apologize   let me thank you for you have been a doll in ignoring all of this   it's strange that you do not punch me while I stand here   no   your blue eyes stare right past me   Barbie eyes filled with wine and gin tonight   scotch tomorrow   stare right past me to the trees in the park   you really can't see me?   I should have known   it's the way it has always been isn't it?   I will go away now   don't worry   I will not even go upstairs to see my beloved   would my stare have to be as blank to keep her?

LAST DAY

It's almost the last day of the month and today I have
been all around the world of our land on my skis and
it was a big sunny land full of powder   the world
was full of what it is like not to see or feel your body
the stench of love   sweet like a coronation   and
sour too   a cut in the mountain down to the septic
pit   the smell of you   shown ass backwards and
naked sitting on a stump of a tree   the fat   the lack
of testicles and hair   the stench you run from   the
power to be seen   revealed   the tell-all   with
nothing left and wiped off the face of the earth

CALL ME

What would it take for you to call me?   just the
craving in my heart?   the recollection of a long walk
up the road as I now walk around the house cleaning
as if you will be here this weekend?   what would
it take for you to stride across the snow?   to plant
you   my heart next to yours on the couch   no
one to invade us   my voice in your ear   all of our
commitments thrown out the window   would it take
my hand?   a night-long seduction?   would it take
sweet music?   a slow fuck?   another woman's
voice?   would it take a rainy day?   a prayer?
would it take a god's intervention to lead you through
the narrow door down the labyrinthine steps to your
basement where you once told me be careful not to
bump my head   to place your index finger on the
phone?   would it take a career?   an acceptance?
the memory of my smell?   desire sucking around
your cunt?   a flat iron?   a slap across the cheeks?
would it take you helping a customer?   walking to
the back of the store and looking down to be struck
by the memory of us there on the floor where I do
not say a word while I make love to your left breast
where I could go on all night and where you stop me
from hurting you   and when I touch you find you very
wet   when you come I fuck you   barely   then
more when you ask and I would not have let you come
so soon had there not been a deadline   your walk
slows down and you forget what you are saying to
your customer while I lift you to the back seat of a
taxicab and take you again as we drive across town

I HAVEN'T

I haven't written to you   I haven't bought a new
car   I haven't talked to my ex-girlfriend   I haven't
bathed   I haven't called   I haven't read a book   I
haven't eaten   I haven't blown up a building   I
haven't painted   I haven't killed   I haven't cut my
nails   I haven't touched myself   I haven't fed the
birds   I haven't gone running   I haven't planted
peas   I haven't written a novel   I haven't looked
for a new job   I haven't blown my nose   I haven't
watched basketball   I haven't gotten you a gift for
your birthday   I haven't fled to Paris   I haven't
cooked rice   I haven't looked for a house   I haven't
slept

I have talked to the angels   I have kissed my yellow
dog   I have thrown a yellow frisbee   I have seen
22 robins   I have watched a movie   I have thought
about dying   I have poured wine for the Seder   I
have given birth   I have grown a beard   I have
vacuumed the couch   I have listened to the dead   I
have watered the plants   I have baked lasagna   I
have built a fire   I have paid my taxes   I have
counted the plagues   I have mailed a letter bomb   I
have dyed my hair   I have left town on my motorcycle

FIRST AND LAST

You will meet me in that hotel and I will blast down the
door   I will drag you across the acrylic carpet and
you will have rug burns for days   meet me there and
I will take you so hard it will be impossible for you ever
to rest again in the quiet of your home   you will be
thrown through the windows and you will know the
tornado   I will crash your feet up against the walls
and you will not fight back   I will have you whole fist
this time and you will not resist and you will have me
you will cry and want and be left and break and not be
able to get on the train or drive away   you will never
walk back into the door of your whispered life and you
will nod and crave and not lie down and acknowledge
and bow and dive and mop up the floors of oceans
you will crawl around your cabin at night   you will
stop planning and start trusting the tracks the path the
tail of comets the pie in the sky the orbits of meteors
you will walk those ways and hear the loudest monk
horn calling at 3:42 a.m. for arousal and golden robes
and you will throw it all off and shout without sense
or kindness and howl and houses will fly through the
air and you will wake up and smell shit and heaven in
your first and very last breath

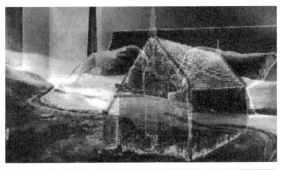

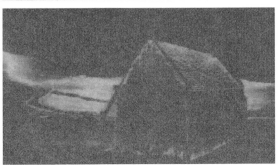

157

Essays

AND THAT I AM ALSO SOME YOUNG BOY*

Ari Banias

I'm in the grey-brown carpeted 811s of the Sarah Lawrence library looking for a book. Someone older and cooler has mentioned it offhandedly, like I should know. It's 1997, I'm 19.

I remember thinking that can't really be the title of a book. What seemed impossible about it? Hearing it, you knew the book was queer. It flagged—but stealthily, using everyday speech. A wink. It signaled mainly with syntax and the intimacy of address. Then, seeing it printed: the *Home,* and the *Don't,* the lowercase rest of it with those definitive periods. The title toggled thrillingly between command and plea and wouldn't sit still.

At 19 I'd read *Doing it for Daddy*, and Marilyn Hacker's sonnet sequences, and a good number of riot grrrl zines, but nothing I had yet encountered in poetry allowed that sensibilities like these could be anything but at odds. I hadn't yet found a queer poetry that made me freeze then flush with recognition. Like seeing another queer person in public see you.

Home in three days. Don't wash. became one of those books that offered a way through the problems of poetic language for me as a young writer trying to render queerness in poems, and as a gender nonconforming person seeking vocabularies for my body and the ways I desired. This was a whole, unapologetic way to be—that you could love and fuck and hurt and obsess and be ordinary with your sink full of dirty dishes and make art of this.

The compressed, breathless scenes in *Home* were unrestrained and specific, sometimes crisp and sometimes pixelated, spliced with detail, but also thick—thick with a hard-to-pinpoint anonymity that tipped past porn and into the territory of the letter, the long-distance call. Something you could hold and smell. Or hear breathing. A face that returned your stare.

> "I will turn you around just before you fall to spread you further   right up into your liver your spleen your chest your heart your lungs until you cannot breathe"

What did it mean to find exhilaration like this in a line? The nearness and force of language willing the body to open, to explode, to turn inside out. It was around then I first started to understand something about my body's capacity for pain. That almost no pain was just pain, and that some of it

159

overlapped with sex, with fantasy. And that ruthlessness and tenderness shared terrain.

∧ ∧ ∧

I'm reading Sam again, two decades later.

> "I will lick you clean   all of that will be mine   I have fasted for days waiting"

Two decades later, the pitch and tenor of desire these poems assert remains threatened, and threatening.

> "I am so far inside you I no longer care if I tear you apart   I am only a part of a hundred trains"

With their determination to follow pleasure and longing past the polite or permissible, even into the near-brutal, Sam's poems speak at what are still the extremities of queer intimacy. This indelible force outlives taste or period or school or style; maybe it's what's queer about queerness. In this poetic restlessness, residues of loves, bad-good decisions, future heart-breaks, and gender feelings aren't just stored, but quite alive.

Sam's poems spoke to a trans me before that word was within my reach. Reading them, I got to feel a way I needed to feel. Into a future. Here, you get to have a cunt and a dick, be boy and girl and neither, forget your cock on the bathroom sink, be doomed to care about someone, find yourself gutted by longing in the boredom of the everyday, like we were, as we do.

I want nothing less than these unsettled relations, full of heart, abject, as they slide backward and forward across time, to where it's possible the ones to come will love so hard "houses will fly through the air."

*the title is taken from the poem "Telephone II"

LINDA SMUKLER'S TRANS POETICS

Cameron Awkward-Rich

I found my way to Linda Smukler's *Normal Sex* by retracing Samuel Ace's steps. I was in search of something like a trans[masculine] poetics, however gauzy, vague. My method: flipping through the pages of *Troubling the Line: Trans and Genderqueer Poetry and Poetics,* gazing at each constellation of name/photograph/text, waiting for that stir of familiarity, the feel of looking into the face of a might-be friend.[1]

In his introduction to the Belladonna* reprint of *Normal Sex / Home in three days. Don't wash.*, Samuel, faced with the gap—of time, of category, of relations—between who he was, writing those books, and who he is now, tasked to account for them, asks, "How does a writer look back?" He approaches an answer by staging a conversation between the present and the past, between Sam and Sam conjuring Linda's voice. As a reader, I have a slightly different question, though one that is also rooted in a preoccupation with categories, with time. Namely, how ought a reader approach a text, knowing what comes after? I found Linda through Sam, after all, and read her work consciously in search of him. Reading this way, *Normal Sex* seemed to me a door she made, through which he, eventually, entered.

When I first encountered Sam in *Troubling the Line*, it was as a photograph of a stern-looking white man in a fedora, a white t-shirt, thick glasses that seemed both to intensify and obscure his gaze. One of the (false) truisms about transmasculine life is that girlhood leaves no trace, which is a way of thinking about time and space that also structures some of the most pernicious American fantasies. At the time, I was living on the edge of a gentrifying area of Oakland with a dear friend who had recently seroconverted, alongside an estimated half of all queer black male-assigned folks. There, in the body of the city and the body of my friend, I could see, daily, the past leaving its mark in the present—the disavowed, ongoing world-making effects of redlining, of government non-response to HIV, of mass incarceration, on and on. While his poems had a music and phrasing that sticks in the head, what I liked most about this Sam in the photograph was that, although he seemed solid enough, he, too, was fixated on ghostlife, on systems of ordering and the modes of looking that are forced upon us/made possible when we fall through their cracks, "*the infinite slide through the river of identitude...* It's been 10 years without a name."[2]

Much of *Normal Sex* is more straightforwardly narrative, but thematizes what Sam's later writing formalizes. In particular, the first two sections of the book add up to a story about a child who, when faced with the impoverishment of and violences thrumming around her everyday world, finds a way to live out a thick fantasy life as a monkey/boy/adventurer in a world adjacent, arrived at through portals opened by music and by fear. *Boyhood*, in this story, is something less like 'gender identity' and more like a reparative retreat into the vast territories of the interior. *Boyhood* names a child's wish and need for the loosening of gender's, of modernity's, of subjectivity's constraints.

Knowing that it was published squarely between Gayle Rubin's 1992 "Of Catamites and Kings: Reflections on Butch, Gender, and Boundaries" and Jack Halberstam's 1998 "Transgender Butch: Butch/FTM Border Wars and the Masculine Continuum," two of the most oft-cited academic dispatches from intra-community disputes over "the meanings of various masculine embodiments," I cannot call *Normal Sex* a transparently 'trans' text.[3] However, I am hopeful this republication will lead to the book being more widely read and understood as central to trans literary history, as it is an intimate—rather than polemic—dispatch from this time in which the "territories of queer gender" were being actively expanded, remapped, and contested.[4] 'Trans,' then, was a possible horizon, but no one could yet point to a body of writing self-consciously called 'trans lit.'

Perhaps for this reason, there is an expansiveness, a searching, and a formal/narrative irresolution to *Normal Sex* that is more difficult to pull off in 2018, now that everyone knows (or, at least, thinks they know) how that story goes. And yet, part of the pleasure and difficulty of reading *Normal Sex* now is that, in a way, we do know how the story goes: Linda's lost boyhood will be recovered, if only a little late. Perhaps paradoxically, then, its too-early arrival allows *Normal Sex* to exemplify an impulse that marks many aesthetic objects we call trans, an impulse that need not have anything to do with gender, per se. Rather, we might think of trans as a particular practice of imagination, a reparative retreat into an expanded inner territory and an insistence that the life of the interior, "where I am the center," *is* a real life.[5]

"Go back now to that boy taken by that girl   there aren't that many who would want to undress him and get beneath the suit jacket and the white shirt… come come now now through the boy through the fingernail dirt back to the girl underneath it all and the comecome nownow sunk and drowned in the great green pond."[6] I confess. I went off searching for you because, newly transforming, I was utterly unmoored. Linda, I did not want to be a man. I wanted to be free.

NOTES

1 Trace Peterson and TC Tolbert, eds., *Troubling the Line: Trans and Genderqueer Poetry and Poetics* (New York: Nightboat Books, 2013).

2 Samuel Ace, "I met a man," in *Troubling the Line: Trans and Genderqueer Poetry and Poetics*, 431.

3 Judith Halberstam, "Transgender Butch: Butch/FTM Border Wars and the Masculine Continuum," *GLQ* 4, no. 2 (1998): 288. See also: Gayle Rubin, "Of Catamites and Kings: Reflections on Butch, Genders, and Boundaries," *The Transgender Studies Reader*, edited by Susan Stryker and Stephen Whittle (New York: Routledge, 2006), 471-481.

4 Halbertsam, 288.

5 Linda Smukler, *Normal Sex* (Ithaca: Firebrand, 1994), 9.

6 Ibid, 84.

MY LETTER OF APPRECIATION

Joan Nestle (Melbourne, Australia)

"Watch how I tell you a story and then tell you the same story so many years later." Yes, Samuel. Yes, Linda. Now you are both back in my life, each with your histories, pointing to a new kind of genderedfull future. It has been many years since I worked with Linda Smukler on the Thursday volunteer nights at the old home of the Lesbian Herstory Archives. Linda with her hat, her suspenders and her slim pants. Her wry smile, her quiet. But it is only so many years later, now, that I read the deeper story both of Linda and of Samuel, the deeper poetic line, the pulsing phrases of old and new positionings, of body, of desire, of complex histories held cupped in Ace's commitment to not let go while time dances around his body, the poetics of change and constancy. I gaze at the author's photograph introducing his brilliant contributions to *Troubling the Line: Trans and Genderqueer Poetry and Poetics* (eds. TC Tolbert and Trace Peterson) and realize we are both old now, that time has carried us much further down the river then I had thought, that I live so deeply in the moments of my own life, trying to be this 78-year-old fem woman, with a faltering body, in a new hemisphere, that I have lost the ability to imagine how time is carving its way on the bodies, on the lines, of long unseen writer friends back in the old country.

These two books bring back the tensions created by the 1970s-onward lesbian feminist urge to take new ground, while at the same time remind me of the punishment that awaited if that ground made other feminists—lesbian and otherwise—uncomfortable. In some ways these are both old and new readings to me: the pain, the anger, the exploration of desires when the body is almost beyond itself, the family betrayals that move into open air, again call up a time when anger born from tortured intimacies took on its own aesthetic. The brilliance of this new creation lies in the letter that Samuel writes to Linda, an exchange between historical selves I have not read before, an exchange I feel privileged to read. I have been uneasy with the growing campaign about lesbian invisibility, with the blaming of transpeople for this so called erasure from history. Linda and Samuel have worked out a way to honor the creative rush of the cultural politics of another time in the midst of yet another cultural transformation, not one replacing the other but embracing the knowledges of both, and in this process, the writing goes deeper into the human journey then I ever thought possible. Samuel and Linda are speaking of the human experience of time, the histories of selves, so easy to leave each other in the night, but because a part of him was always a part of her, they break the borders open. This is the creation of a new writing ethics of multigendered selves, mapping with respect and sometimes love, that which made self possible.

Dear Gloria Anzaldúa, old friend, in the warmth of your riven self, in your knowledge of the lands in between, you gave life to Linda and Samuel, from the '70s to here, and they carry it into new times, such desperate times where the ability to love beyond the borders maybe the only thing that saves us.

ENCOUNTERING SAM ACE

Andrea Lawlor

I first encountered Samuel Ace's work when I was in high school (in the special 1989 "Diversity/Adversity" issue of *Ploughshares*, edited by Marilyn Hacker). Sam's well known poem "Monkey Boy" appeared there for the first time, and it was through this little volume (still on my shelf) that I realized queer and gender-noncomforming people wrote poetry, were writers.

But I didn't actually meet Sam Ace until many years later. I first heard him read in 2013 at the AWP writers' conference in Boston. Sam's performance of his work and discussion of his process on the Writing Masculinities panel was mesmerizing; I followed him around like a puppy, catching him again later that night at the launch party for *Troubling the Line: Trans and Genderqueer Poetry*, the anthology that introduced his work to a new generation of readers.

Troubling the Line is an important touchstone, for me at least, for thinking about Sam's career, an activity I do with some regularity. The work in Sam's first two volumes of poetry, *Normal Sex* (1994) and *Home in three days. Don't wash.* (1996) prefigures his later experiments with form and sound. *Normal Sex*, for instance, consists entirely of prose poems, a poetic form of in-betweenness. The original 1996 printing of *Home in three days. Don't wash.* came with a CD-ROM. This early work, though lavishly praised by queer critics like Felice Picano and Rebecca Brown, was also controversial in some quarters—certain lesbian feminist readers, ironically, found the representations of non-normative sexuality and gender identity *too* non-normative, too challenging of the gender essentialism so prevalent at that time. Fortunately, most readers disagreed, and many younger poets like Ari Banias cite Sam's early work as crucial to their development as poets.

In fact, the poet Trace Peterson uses Sam's early work to articulate a "trans poetry aesthetic." Peterson describes three characteristics of this aesthetic: first, the poems avoid "directly presenting a narrative about being trans"; secondly, they "destabilize... an idealized sense of self in the articulation of that self... [by] explor[ing] experimental linguistic strategies"; and third, they "push the borders of genre, writing a kind of poetry-within-prose relying on 'gaps' or leaps that suggest ghostly line breaks" (Peterson 524).

Sam has always worked in multiple media, has always questioned genre and disciplinary boundaries, as well as calcified ideas about life trajectories. He began his artistic career as a classical musician, then went to graduate school at Yale to study painting, then, poetry. Sam's career is, for me, a model of possibility for queer art-making, for trans life-making.

The poet Joy Ladin says that Ace's work "presents trans identity… as a vector of possibility," a "syntax that individual readers can use to make sense of ourselves and our lives" (np). Sam's work is a model of collaboration and generosity, like Sam himself. I am so grateful for his presence, his kindness, and his living example of how to make work that finds its audience *because* of its refusal to compromise.

Now Sam's office is right next to mine, in a ramshackle little white house on a sleepy college campus in Massachusetts. I often corner him in the hall and ask advice, cadge stories about his youth, try to steer the conversation around to Gloria Anzaldúa (okay, I only did that once). I don't understand how time works, how we're both who we were in 1989 and who we are now, and I'm frankly astounded to have had the good fortune to be befriended by this lovely man. To have the poems would have been enough—but I'm so greedy. Thank you, Sam!

WORKS CITED

Joy Ladin, "I Am Not Me: Unmaking and Remaking the Language of the Self," Lambda Literary, December 28, 2014, https://www.lambdaliterary.org/features/12/28/unmaking-and-remaking-the-language-of-the-self/.

Trace Peterson, "Becoming a Trans Poet: Samuel Ace, Max Wolf Valerio, and kari edwards," *TSQ* 1, no. 4 (2014): 523-538.

EMBODYING TIME

Yanyi

One is trans before transitioning, before calling oneself trans, before consciousness is pinned to language. Between one's then and now, before passing, time passes. Ace/Smukler's work is a search for lost time. "Tales of a Lost Boyhood" in *Normal Sex* blur into the furtive time stolen by cheating lovers in *Home in three days. Don't wash.* Writing emerges as a way of regaining time never passed, as well as a way to reify time that has passed. "The act of writing these stories fixes them in time," Ace writes to Smukler in their interlocuting letters. "Unlike actual people and relationships, these portraits do not evolve."

The double resonance of this statement lies in that Smukler's poems run right through all kinds of trauma, from childhood sexual abuse to gender dysphoria experienced through the eyes of a young trans boy in "Tales of a Lost Boyhood." The stories of trauma, too, keep reenacting themselves in loops. But in looking back at Smukler's work, Ace is "faced with a person [he] no longer fully [recognizes]," wondering if he could or would write the same poems he did twenty years ago. Transitions happen all the time. Yet, changes in one's body require time to pass, and that difference becomes tethered to a particular moment with no simple way to extricate the process of evolving one's gender from evolving one's humanity. "Dear friend who is me and no longer me, dear love who I have never left behind, dear gorgeous Linda, in all that your name implies, let me say again that I love you."

What feels particular to my own transition in this work is how Ace and Smukler express that desire to recapture lost time, catching up to— or finally inhabiting—a body that is both concrete, dynamic, and exactly mine, not just frozen within myself or within a story of myself. The letters that begin this book are not just correspondences, but declarations of love, and love is what binds Ace to Smukler across embodied time. The common term we have for a name no longer in use, usually a gendered given name, is "deadname." Deadname is both a noun and a verb, a descriptor as well as an invocation. But instead of the invocation of a muse, Ace revives Smukler, seeing both a *you* and *me* in the mirror who are worth pursuing and holding in the present. "I want to locate myself with you, integrated and whole," Ace explains.

Between Samuel Ace and Linda Smukler, between my past self and my future self, the space wedged by time and bodies seems to stretch too far to ever recuperate and hold at once. Yet, this space is what triggers the magnitude of propulsion toward repair. Between Ace and Smukler, whether it is he or she who speaks, what is most enduring is that radical generosity, the shared tenacity to write each other, alive.

PRAYER FOR US, IN THE WILDERNESS

TC Tolbert

In 1998, about 5 years before I started (acknowledged?) my lifelong gender transition, I took a Wilderness First Responder course—emergency medicine for the backcountry—10 days of fake-blood scenarios complete with running through the night and rescue equipment culled from gear we'd likely be carrying in the field. While I learned a lot about cleaning wounds, splinting broken arms, and pulling traction on femur fractures (that last one is a practice that is now frowned upon), the most provoking lesson was this: *never create a 2nd victim.* It's simple, decent guidance. Everyone nods along when they hear it—*yes, yes, don't hurt yourself or someone else by going in there unprepared.* Then suddenly you're standing at the cliff's edge, watching a body tumbling down and all you want to do is get under it. You realize how little instinct you carry, perhaps especially in a crisis, to keep yourself safe.

I first read *Meet Me There* (as individual books) in 2007. I was desperate for trans connection and poetry and a new way to build family. I'd been running into every burning building of a relationship I could find hoping to either double the fire, find a hero, or be one—covered in acne, taking in and spilling new hormones at 33. Just a few years younger than my father, the first grown trans-man poet I'd ever met, Sam and his poems quickly began to befriend me.

"What would the houses say?" he asked. And for years I wrote about architecture when I thought about killing myself or just making myself disappear. Watching Sam's vulnerability and generosity, how he works carefully to keep these approaches collaborative instead of competitive—"I close my eyes, but then I have to see"—I began to get closer to my own body, to write about my abuse history and also my love for Melissa and the life/body from which she grew into TC.

Reading *Meet Me There* now, I can see how much I've turned to Sam's writing in the last 11 years not to save me, exactly, but to mentor me. Mentoring in the purest sense of the word—someone who thinks with purpose and spirit, someone who allows this thinking to be witnessed. Thanks to this mentorship, I am learning how to visit the wildernesses of trauma, gender, love, sex, and poetry prepared to be courageous while at the same time valuing my own safety. I am reminded that my heart is part of my body. I am learning to recognize the body falling from the cliff as my own, as well as the body terrified and the one working to heal and fighting to feel safe. Perhaps I'm most excited for this re-publication because I don't think I'm the only trans-person who will be sustained by Sam's work in this way.

Responding to and engaging with the crisis and deep desire of being a person with a body and a history—without creating a second victim—seems to be the bedrock of Sam's poetics. Present and porous, full of music, capable while recognizing one's lack of control. I think of this poetic practice as not only life-saving, but life-giving. How grateful I am to be shaped by Sam and his writing.

May every trans writer find sanctuary, wherever there is wilderness in this world.

HUNGRY

Pamela Sneed

The introduction of Samuel Ace's *Normal Sex* and *Home in three days. Don't wash.* breaks my heart and ravishes me. It ravishes me with its beauty of language, experimentation in form both poetry and poetics, its necessity and its conversation between two selves, letters where one self is not necessarily left behind to form another, but the former self is acknowledged and in dialogue with the other, the ones they've become. I cried hearing the path that Sam, a trans and genderqueer writer and visual artist has forged to become themselves, the families and the communities that can sometimes be lost in the urgency to speak and live one's truth, and the poet's everlasting commitment to speak to honor themselves, and to forge ahead despite loss and sacrifices. Even before their name was mentioned I heard Dorothy Allison in the opening essay of *Trash* titled "Deciding to Live," where she describes sitting in a motel room writing her story on yellow legal pads, determined to get it all down and how writing was part of her stubborn decision to live. I can see Gloria Anzaldúa, co-editor of the anthology *This Bridge Called my Back* (a book which saved my life) and her lasting legacy of organizing and giving space to lesbian writers / encouraging them to speak. You can see that Sam and Linda's work is in the tradition and spirit of Allison and Anzaldúa's work as well.

It's without a doubt reading *Normal Sex* and *Home in three days. Don't wash.* this is still pioneering work / to document lesbian desire / trans desire. I can't stop thinking about the time period that these works were first published / when lesbian desire / trans desire and sex were not often talked about / certainly not depicted in words truthfully in all their danger and redemption / the early days when we did not see ourselves in literature and still don't often enough. I think about the terrible damning repression of Senator Jesse Helms and the lasting scars of the Reagan administration long into the '90s and even in our own communities who lived in fear and subsequently repressed each other. I think about the AIDS era and losing so many of our queer brothers men of color and white men and how difficult it was to break and fight through silence. *Home in three days. Don't wash.* is rife with the personal and political, meaning don't wash / don't erase / don't sanitize my truth our truth and then the rise to personal power, "I will lick you clean, all of that will be mine." In America, in 2018 we are living under a dangerous and fascist

172

regime, and desire and language that falls outside the mainstream is forbidden / marginalized / shut out, once again this work comes at a time when it is most needed.

I can only say in finality, reading these works I realize how hungry I am / have always been for these words / how they are timeless and never stop being brave words and works. I am proud of Sam Ace and Belladonna* for bringing this work forward for a new generation that is starving to hear.

PHILOSOPHY IN THE WATER CLOSET

Kay Gabriel

What does writing sex do that visual porn can't? Sam Ace: "I want the same underwear the same sour smell layers of it thick the soak and musk of you."[1] I think about a guy I went down on in high school, unremarkable sex but then I'd leave his place washed in the pulpy smell of his cum. Sam gets his fingers slick and lodges them under your nose. Smell is almost anti-pornographic, if "pornography" means watching a hygienic fuck in a scene without shit. But why should it? The narrator of "Trash" rolls a used condom off a strap-on and chews on it, "I tasted latex and lubricant and I tasted you."[2] That's intriguing, right? Like watching some-body else eat: the eggs burst and dribble down a bit. Do you want some?

Home in three days. Don't wash. sits only at the edge of pornogra-phy, focused more on the afterimage or anticipation of an illicit fuck than the scene itself. The sex—the affair, is that tawdry?—happens over the phone until a motel meetup. A poetry of smells is like giving you a key to the room and showing you upstairs. Actually, tawdriness is kind of the point. In the 19th-century realist novel Fredric Jameson uncovers the devel-opment of a "new and autonomous realm of the sensory,"[3] the redolent world of smell. For Jameson the antonym of this "dizzying continuity of smells"[4] is cleanliness, a class-coded aesthetic of mastery over sensations, putrescence, losing your wallet. So an erotics of smell—cunt, ass, sweat, food, trash and shit—promises to restore a full and disalienated body, but only in light of the bourgeois ideology that breaks that body into various bits and capacities in the first place, consigning smell to the rarefied realm of experience. For stink to become meaningful, which is to say sexual, it had to pass through the digestive tract of propriety and come out the other side. Still, why hang out there in the hallway?

Maybe you'd hang back if you were on the wrong, the anti-pornography, side of the lesbian sex wars. (Does it make sense to continue taking sides in that fight? So long as some feminists moralize, to sometimes devastating effect, against sex work and trans people—that is to say, so long as the most harmful residues of anti-porn feminism persist—I'd say so.) You can see evidence of that conflict in Sam's writing, which takes sides as ferociously as anything. On the one hand, *Home in three days* operates under a moral economy: in the epigraph Sam gives the collection, Reinaldo Arenas threatens "years of sorrow for every moment of pleasure." On the other, Sam shrugs off moral dictates like open shirts:

"I put my cock to your throat when you are a man and I am a little boy and you suck me off when you are a woman, my mother humiliating me with dresses and stockings."[5] Taboos impose themselves the better to sustain the pleasure of their fantasized transgression. No morals left standing, just the feeling that animates play, a quasi-religious fervor of the senses. Maybe that's 'cause moralizing about fucking and fantasy—like merritt k says, a "total mood killer"[6]—makes for a useless non-politics in the first place. Sam promises you'll "wake up and smell shit and heaven."[7] Are you in, or what?

NOTES

1 Linda Smukler, *Home in three days. Don't wash.* (West Stockbridge, MA: Hard Press, 1996), 43. [*Meet Me There*, 119.]
2 Ibid., 15. [*Meet Me There*, 101.]
3 Fredric Jameson, *Antinomies of Realism* (New York and London: Verso, 2013), 55.
4 Ibid.
5 *Home in three days. Don't wash.*, 75. [*Meet Me There*, 141.]
6 merritt k, "How to Love in Precarious Times," in merritt k and Niina Pollari, *Total Mood Killer* (TigerBee Press, 2017).
7 *Home in three days. Don't wash.*, 93. [*Meet Me There*, 152.]

MONDAY

Eileen Myles

It seems like the great contribution of trans identity to this moment in time is the practical buttressing of the notion of self as multiple. I knew Linda and I knew the work of Linda Smukler and I know Sam Ace and know his work. I've met them all at junctures great and small and the support and inspiration I've gleaned from any of them is abiding. The person and the work were never same and then they are in swift and awesome flexible moments of transparency. The literature that functions like a joint welcomes everyone not to say I'm just like you but that you too can witness the grandeur of nature and evolution in art that is always epochal like their work is. It's no accident that Linda worked in a hybrid form which seems like an old-fashioned word now for poetry that looks forward and back up and down inside and out at once. Today in my car in alternate parking for an hour and a half I hold the pain and the beauty of the city while I sit with my friend and love them.

CONTRIBUTORS

Samuel Ace is a trans and genderqueer poet and sound artist, and the author of several books, most recently *Our Weather Our Sea*, (Black Radish Books, 2019). He is the recipient of the Astraea Lesbian Writers and Firecracker Alternative Book awards, as well as a two-time finalist for both the Lambda Literary Award and the National Poetry Series. Recent work can be found in *Poetry, PEN America, Best American Experimental Poetry,* and many other journals and anthologies. He currently teaches poetry and creative writing at Mount Holyoke College in western Massachusetts.

Cameron Awkward-Rich is the author of *Sympathetic Little Monster* (Ricochet Editions, 2016) and *Dispatch* (Persea Books, 2019). He received his Ph.D. in Modern Thought and Literature from Stanford University and is currently an Assistant Professor of Women, Gender, Sexuality Studies at the University of Massachusetts Amherst.

Ari Banias is the author of *Anybody* (W.W. Norton, 2016). He is the recipient of fellowships from the New York Foundation for the Arts, the Fine Arts Work Center in Provincetown, the Wisconsin Institute for Creative Writing, and Stanford University. Ari lives in Berkeley and teaches in the Bay Area.

Kay Gabriel is the author of *Elegy Department Spring / Candy Sonnets 1* (BOAAT Press, 2017), the finalist for the 2016 BOAAT Chapbook Prize selected by Richard Siken. She's a PhD candidate at Princeton University and a 2018-19 Emerge-Surface-Be Fellow at the Poetry Project.

Andrea Lawlor teaches writing, edits fiction for *Fence,* and has been awarded fellowships by Lambda Literary and Radar Labs. Their writing has appeared in various literary journals including *Ploughshares, jubilat,* the *Brooklyn Rail, Faggot Dinosaur,* and *Encyclopedia, Vol. II.* Their publications include a chapbook, *Position Papers* (Factory Hollow Press, 2016), and a novel, *Paul Takes the Form of a Mortal Girl* (Rescue Press, 2017).

Eileen Myles is a poet, novelist, and art journalist. Their twenty-one books include *evolution, Afterglow (a dog memoir),* a 2017 re-issue of *Cool for*

You and *I Must Be Living Twice/new and selected poems*, and *Chelsea Girls*. They teach at NYU and Naropa and live in NYC and Marfa, TX.

Joan Nestle is a Bronx-born (1940) anti-Occupation Jew, anti-Trump lesbian, co-Founder of the Lesbian Herstory Archives (1974-), author of *A Restricted Country* (1988) and *A Fragile Union* (1998), editor of *The Persistent Desire: A Fem-Butch Reader*, and co-editor of *GenderQueer: Beyond the Binary*, with Riki Wilchins and Clare Howell. Above all, grateful to all my comrades who stand with bodies bared against the rise of Fascism.

Pamela Sneed is a New York-based poet, writer, performer and emerging visual artist. She is author of *Imagine Being More Afraid of Freedom than Slavery, KONG and Other Works,* and a chaplet, "Gift" by Belladonna*. Her work is widely anthologized and appears in Nikki Giovanni's, "The 100 Best African American Poems." Her book *Sweet Dreams* was published by Belladonna* in 2018.

TC Tolbert often identifies as a trans and genderqueer feminist, collaborator, dancer, and poet. And, s/he's a human in love with humans doing human things. S/he is Tucson's Poet Laureate and author of *Gephyromania* (Ahsahta Press 2014), 4 chapbooks, and co-editor of *Troubling the Line: Trans and Genderqueer Poetry and Poetics* (Nightboat Books 2013).

Yanyi is associate editor at Foundry and the recipient of fellowships from Asian American Writers' Workshop and Poets House. He won the 2018 Yale Series of Younger Poets prize, awarded by Carl Phillips, for *The Year of Blue Water* (Yale University Press, 2019). Find him at yanyiii.com.

ACKNOWLEDGEMENTS

I am forever grateful to the Belladonna* Collective for bringing my little books back into the world. As an author, I could not be more thankful for the team that worked so collaboratively with me on this project. Rachael Wilson, Maxe Crandall, Jean Lee, Jack Henrie Fisher—you have been a dream to work with over these months. I bow to you for all of your brilliance and effort. Rachel Levitsky, thank you always, for your heart, your willingness, and your support.

Thank you Nancy Bereano at Firebrand Books, Jonathan Gams and Susan Levin at Hard Press, for having the faith to first publish my books.

I am very grateful to the following institutions who, many years ago, provided much needed material and spiritual support for the work: The Millay Colony, the Edward F. Albee Foundation, the Astraea Lesbian Foundation for Justice, the Lesbian Herstory Archives, the WOW Café Theater, the Lambda Literary Foundation, the City College of New York, the New York Foundation for the Arts. Also to the publishers and editors of journals and anthologies where many of the poems first appeared. *Sinister Wisdom, Conditions, On Our Backs, Gay and Lesbian Poetry in Our Time, The World in Us, The New Fuck You*, and so many others;

still alive in my heart, the friends, mentors, and teachers who were there, now gone: Gloria Anzaldúa, Carl Morse, Sonny Wainwright, Essex Hemphill, Robert Giard, Audre Lorde, Mabel Hampton, Assoto Saint; many who were with me at the time, and are still here—writing, fighting, living and loving: Marilyn Hacker, Deb Edel, Morgan Gwenwald, Dorothy Varon, Sarah Schulman, Holly Hughes, Paula Grant, Hilary Sio, Susan Fox Rogers, Amber Hollibaugh, Susie Bright, Trace Peterson, Cheryl Clarke, Jewelle Gomez, Dorothy Allison, Maureen Seaton, Sonny Nordmarken, Trish Salah.

for your love and the new consideration you've given to these words: CA Conrad, Ely Shipley, Kevin Killian, Joan Larkin, Michelle Tea, Cam Awkward-Rich, Kay Gabriel, Eileen Myles, Pamela Sneed, Andrea Lawlor, Joan Nestle, TC Tolbert, Yanyi, Ari Banias.

More than you know, your presence, your work, your lives, continue to nourish me.

"The Roads" was first published in *The Equalizer: Third Series*, edited by Michael Schiavo, in 2018.

Normal Sex was originally published by Firebrand Editions in Ithaca, NY in 1994.

Home in three days. Don't wash. was originally published by Hard Press in West Stockbridge, MA in 1996.

Many of the poems in this volume were first published (some in slightly different versions) in the following anthologies and periodicals: *13th Moon, The American Voice, The Arc of Love, Best American Erotica: 1996, Best Lesbian Erotica, Conditions, Gay and Lesbian Poetry in Our Time* (St. Martin's), *Girlfriends, Global City, Kenyon Review, Lingo, The Little Magazine* (cd-rom), *Love's Shadow* (Crossing Press), *A Movement of Eros, Naming The Waves: Contemporary Lesbian Poetry* (Virago), *New England Review/Bread Loaf Quarterly, The New Fuck You: Adventures in Lesbian Reading, Out the Other Side: Contemporary Lesbian Poetry* (Virago), *Ploughshares, The Prose Poem: An International Journal, Semiotext(e) USA, Sinister Wisdom, The Women's Times*, and *The Zenith of Desire*.

Meet Me There: Normal Sex & Home in three days. Don't wash.
Samuel Ace / Linda Smukler

Copyright © 2019 Samuel Ace
ISBN: 978-0-9988439-2-6

Cover design by Rachael Guynn Wilson
Interior images by Samuel Ace

Belladonna* is a reading and publication series that promotes the work of women*-identified and queer feminist writers who are adventurous, experimental, politically involved, multiform, multicultural, multi-gendered, impossible to define, unpredictable, and dangerous with language.

This book has been made possible in part by the New York State Council on the Arts, the Leslie Scalapino - O Books Fund, and donations for individuals. Belladonna* is a proud member of CLMP.

Library of Congress Cataloging-in-Publication Data

Names: Ace, Samuel, 1954- author. | Ace, Samuel, 1954- Normal sex. | Ace, Samuel, 1954- Home in three days, don't wash.
Title: Meet me there : Normal sex and Home in three days, don't wash / by Samuel Ace ; Linda Smukler.
Description: Brooklyn, New York : Belladonna Series, 2019.
Identifiers: LCCN 2018053263 | ISBN 9780998843926 (alk. paper)
Subjects: LCSH: Ace, Samuel, 1954---Criticism and interpretation.
Classification: LCC PS3551.C35 A6 2019 | DDC 811/.54--dc23
LC record available at https://lccn.loc.gov/2018053263

Distributed by Small Press Distribution
1341 Seventh Street
Berkeley, CA 94710
spdbooks.org

also available directly through
Belladonna* Series
925 Bergen Street, Suite 405
Brooklyn, NY 11238
belladonnaseries.org

*deadly nightshade, a cardiac and respiratory stimulant, having purplish-red flowers and black berries